Dieter Fensel

Ontologies:
A Silver Bullet for Knowledge Management and Electronic Commerce

Second Edition, Revised and Extended

Foreword by Michael L. Brodie

With 48 Figures

 Springer

Prof. Dr. Dieter Fensel

Universität Innsbruck
Institut für Informatik
Technikerstr. 25
6020 Innsbruck, Austria
and
National University of Ireland, Galway
Digital Enterprise Research Institute (DERI)
University Road
Galway, Ireland
dieter.fensel@uibk.ac.at

Cataloging-in-Publication Data applied for

A catalog record for this book is available from the Library of Congress.

Bibliographic information published by Die Deutsche Bibliothek.
Die Deutsche Bibliothek lists this publication in the Deutsche
Nationalbibliografie; detailed bibliographic data is available in the
Internet at http://dnb.ddb.de.

ACM Subject Classification (1998): I.2, H.3-4, H.5.3, K.4.3, J.2

ISBN 3-540-00302-9 Springer-Verlag Berlin Heidelberg New York

ISBN 3-540-41602-1 1st edition Springer-Verlag Berlin Heidelberg New York

Springer-Verlag Berlin Heidelberg New York,
a member of BertelsmannSpringer Science+Business Media GmbH

springeronline.com

© Springer-Verlag Berlin Heidelberg 2004
Printed in Germany

The use of general descriptive names, registered names, trademarks, etc. in this publication does not imply,
even in the absence of a specific statement, that such names are exempt from the relevant protective laws
and regulations and therefore free for general use.

Typesetting: Author's data
Production: LE-TeX Jelonek, Schmidt & Vöckler GbR, Leipzig
Cover Design: KünkelLopka Werbeagentur GmbH, Heidelberg
Printed on acid-free paper   45/3142YL - 5 4 3 2 1 0

Foreword

"Despite the dotcom boom and bust, the computer and telecommunications revolution has barely begun. Over the next few decades, the Internet and related technologies really will profoundly transform society."[1]

By 2050 the Internet will have impacted our business, culture, and society as a whole as much if not more than did Gutenberg's printing press 600 years ago in 1450. Sheer economics will force the majority of business and government interactions to be automated. Although the rate and extent of automation will vary by domain, most interactions will not only take place over the Web, they will be almost entirely free of human interaction. As with previous industrial revolutions, the profound impacts are unpredictable, especially the social, political, and religious impacts. However, the automation of everyday personal, commercial, and governmental activities is more easily predicted due to the potential economic benefits and the extrapolation of existing automation. The Third Industrial Revolution, the Information/Biotech Revolution, is well underway.

Typically, there are multiple alternative technologies on which next-generation technologies might be built. Currently there are only two widely accepted enabling technologies that are both new, and hence are in their infancy, and mission critical. They are Web Services and the Web, or the next-generation Web, called the Semantic Web. To achieve even some of the promises for these technologies, we must develop vastly improved solutions for addressing the Grand Challenge of Information Technology, namely dealing better with semantics or real-world "meaning". More precisely, we must enhance automated actions and data to more closely correspond to the real-world actions and facts that they represent, with minimal human involvement. This Grand Challenge is the core challenge not just of Information Technology but also of all next-generation automated applications. This challenge has been calling out for a Silver Bullet since the beginning of modern programming.

---

[1] David Manasian: Digital Dilemmas: A survey of the Internet, *The Economist*, January 25, 2003.

So what is a Silver Bullet? The ancient Greeks believed in the mystical power of silver as an infallible defense, means of attack, or solution to an otherwise insoluble problem. Germanic folklore of the Middle Ages held that only silver could slay man-eating werewolves. In a popular late-nineteenth-century English novel a silver bullet was the only means of killing the werewolf that plagued London. In a myth from my youth, the Lone Ranger TV series, based on 1930–40s novels, starred the Lone Ranger, a masked, clean, and heroic vigilante who came to the defense of many a prairie town by using a single silver bullet to slay the villain. The term Silver Bullet entered into the computing vernacular in 1987[2] when "Silver Bullet" was used pejoratively to dismiss the potential of a simple or single solution to longstanding and otherwise invincible software engineering challenges.

"Ontologies: A Silver Bullet for Knowledge Management and Electronic Commerce" provides a comprehensive introduction to the only known potential Silver Bullet for the Grand Challenge. That Silver Bullet is ontologies. An ontology, in the sense used in this book, is a community-mediated and accepted description of the kinds of entities that are in a domain of discourse and how they are related. They provide meaning, organization, taxonomy, agreement, common understanding, vocabulary, and a connection to the "real world". For a given community, dealing with an agreed-upon domain (e.g., selling software over the Web), the ontological solution provides a definition of all required concepts and their relationships so that every program, Web service, or database that solves a problem in that domain can automatically communicate with other like entities based on the common definitions. Such solutions require concepts, languages, and tools, many still in their infancy. This volume gives a comprehensive introduction to ontologies in the context of the Semantic Web and Web Services challenges that lie at the heart of the Next Generation of computing. It describes and illustrates the basic concepts, languages, and tools currently available and in development. It illustrates these with knowledge management and electronic-commerce applications. One application, selling software over the Web, is based on UN/SPSC, an ontology that is accepted and used worldwide. Hence, the applications in this volume are not just speculative. They solve real problems. What is speculative is the adoption and development of ontological concepts, languages, and tools to extend such solutions to all domains. Unlike most technological solutions, ontologies start with human, community agreement on an ontology. Hence, ontologies are not solely a technical challenge. This is what you should expect of a technical solution that connects to the real world as ontologies do, by definition.

---

[2] Frederick P. Brooks: "No Silver Bullet – Essence and Accidents of Software Engineering", *IEEE Computer,* 20(4):10–19, April 1987.

It remains to be seen whether ontologies will be the Silver Bullet for Knowledge Management and Electronic Commerce as this volume suggests or whether ontologies will be just another failed claim for a next-generation technology. To become versed in this, the Grand Challenge of Information Technology, and to understand the challenges and potential solutions that ontologies, and currently only ontologies, offer, you must understand the material offered comprehensively in this volume. The Third Industrial Revolution has begun and ontologies offer the hope of a Silver Bullet to overcome the Grand Challenge that stands in the way of its realization.

White Stallion Ranch Communications   Michael L. Brodie
Tucson, AZ, USA   Chief Scientist
February, 2003   Verizon

Table of Contents

1 Introduction

Recently, ontologies have moved from a topic in philosophy to a topic in applied artificial intelligence that is at the center of modern computer science. Tim Berners-Lee, Director of the World Wide Web Consortium, referred to the future of the current WWW as the *Semantic Web* – an extended Web of machine-readable information and automated services that extend far beyond current capabilities. The explicit representation of the semantics underlying data, programs, pages, and other Web resources will enable a knowledge-based Web that provides a qualitatively new level of service. Automated services will improve in their capacity to assist humans in achieving their goals by "understanding" more of the content on the Web, and thus providing more accurate filtering, categorization, and searches of information sources. This process will ultimately lead to an extremely knowledgeable system that features various specialized reasoning services. These services will support us in nearly all aspects of our daily life – making access to information as pervasive, and necessary, as access to electricity is today.

The backbone technology for this Semantic Web is *ontologies*. Ontologies provide a shared understanding of certain domains that can be communicated between people and application systems. Ontologies are formal structures supporting knowledge sharing and reuse. They can be used to represent explicitly the semantics of structured and semistructured information enabling sophisticated automatic support for acquiring, maintaining, and accessing information. As this is at the center of recent problems in knowledge management, enterprise application integration, and e-commerce, increasing interest in ontologies is not surprising. Therefore, a number of books have recently been published to cover this area. Examples are [Davies et al., 2003], [Fensel et al., 2002(a)], [Fensel et al., 2003], [Gomez Perez & Benjamins, 2002], and [Maedche, 2002]. However, these other publications are either collections of papers written by a diverse group of authors or they focus on a specific aspect of ontologies, for example, ontology learning. The book *Ontologies: A Silver Bullet for Knowledge Management and Electronic Commerce* is one of the few single-authored books that provide comprehensive and concise introductions to the field. The first edition had the merit of being the first book that introduced this area to a broader audience. Compared to the first edition, three major improvements have been made for the second edition:

- Many recent trends in languages, tools, and applications have been integrated and the material has been updated quite substantially, reflecting the dynamics of our area of interest.

- The book is clearly structured into four sections: the concepts underlying ontologies; the languages used to define ontologies; the tool to work with ontologies; and the application areas of ontologies.

- Many small mistakes have been eliminated from the text.

Chapter 2 provides a definition of ontologies and illustrates various aspects of ontologies. Chapter 3 provides a survey of ontology languages, especially in the context of the Web and the Semantic Web. Chapter 4 provides examples of all relevant aspects that arise when working with ontologies. Even commercial tool sets have become available and are described in this chapter. Finally, no technology without its applications. Chapter 5 discusses the application of ontologies in areas such as knowledge management, enterprise application integration, and e-commerce.

All that remains is for me to wish the reader enjoyment and entertainment while reading about one of the most exciting areas of computer science today.

2 Concept

Ontologies were developed in artificial intelligence to facilitate *knowledge sharing and reuse*. Since the beginning of the nineties ontologies have become a popular research topic, investigated by several artificial intelligence research communities, including knowledge engineering, natural-language processing and knowledge representation. More recently, the notion of ontology is also becoming widespread in fields such as intelligent information integration, cooperative information systems, information retrieval, electronic commerce, and knowledge management. The growing popularity of ontologies is in a large part due to what they promise: a shared understanding of some domain that can be communicated between people and application systems. Currently computers are changing from single isolated devices to entry points into a worldwide network of information exchange and business transactions. Therefore support in the exchange of data, information, and knowledge is becoming the key issue in current computer technology. Providing shared domain structures is becoming essential, and ontologies will therefore become a key asset in describing the structure and semantics of information exchange.

Ontologies have been developed to provide a machine-processable semantics of information sources that can be communicated between different agents (software and humans). Many definitions of ontologies have been given in the last decade, but one that, in our opinion, best characterizes the essence of an ontology is based on the related definitions in [Gruber, 1993]: *An ontology is a formal, explicit specification of a shared conceptualization.* A "conceptualization" refers to an abstract model of some phenomenon in the world which identifies the relevant concepts of that phenomenon. "Explicit" means that the type of concepts used and the constraints on their use are explicitly defined. "Formal" refers to the fact that the ontology should be machine readable. Thus different degrees of formality are possible. Large ontologies like WordNet provide a thesaurus over 100,000 natural language terms explained in natural language (see also [Meersman, 2000] for a discussion of this issue). At the other end of the spectrum is Cyc, which provides formal axiomizing theories for many aspects of common-sense knowledge. "Shared" reflects the notion that an ontology captures consensual knowledge, that is, it is not restricted to some individual, but accepted by a group. Basically, the role of ontologies in the knowledge engineering process is to facilitate the construction of a domain model. An ontology provides a vocabulary of terms and relations with which to model the domain. Because ontologies aim at consensual domain knowledge their development is often a cooperative process involving different people, possibly at different locations. People who agree to accept an ontology are said to *commit* themselves to that ontology.

Ontologies are introduced to facilitate knowledge sharing and reuse between various agents, regardless of whether they are human or artificial in nature. They are supposed to offer this service by providing a consensual and formal conceptualization of a certain area. In a nutshell, ontologies are formal and consensual specifications of conceptualizations that provide a shared understanding of a domain, an understanding that can be communicated across people and application systems. Thus, ontologies glue together two essential aspects that help to bring the Web to its full potential:

- Ontologies define formal semantics for information, thus allowing information processing by a computer.

- Ontologies define real-world semantics, which makes it possible to link machine-processable content with meaning for humans based on consensual terminologies.

The latter aspect in particular is still far from having been studied to its full extent: how can ontologies be used to communicate real-world semantics between human and artificial agents? In answering this question we wish to point out two important features of ontologies: they must have a network architecture and they must be dynamic.

Heterogeneity in space or ontology as networks of meaning. From the very beginning, heterogeneity has been an essential requirement for this ontology network. Tools for dealing with conflicting definitions and strong support in interweaving local theories are essential in order to make this technology workable and scalable. Islands of meaning must be interwoven to form more complex structures enabling exchange of information beyond domain, task, and sociological boundaries. This implies two tasks. First, tool support must be provided to define local domain models that express a commitment of a group of agents that share a certain domain and task and that can agree on a joint world-view for this purpose. Second, these local models must be interwoven with other models, such as the social practice of the agents that use ontologies to facilitate their communicational needs. Little work has been done in this latter area. We no longer talk about a single ontology, but rather about a network of ontologies. Links must be defined between these ontologies and this network must allow overlapping ontologies with conflicting – and even contradictory – conceptualizations.

Development in time or living ontologies. Originally, an ontology was intended to reflect the "truth" of a certain aspect of reality. It was the holy task of the philosopher to find such truth. Today, ontologies are used as a means of exchanging meaning between different agents. They can only provide this if they reflect an inter-subjective consensus. By definition, they can only be the result of a social process. This gives ontologies a dual status for the exchange of meaning:

- Ontologies as prerequisite for consensus: Agents can only exchange meaning when they have already agreed on a joint body of meaning reflecting a consensual point of view on the world.

- Ontologies as a result of consensus: Ontologies as consensual models of meaning can only arise as the result of a process where agents agree on a certain model of the world and its interpretation.

Thus, ontologies are as much a prerequisite for consensus and information sharing as they are the results of them. An ontology is as much required for the exchange of meaning as the exchange of meaning may influence and modify an ontology. Consequently, *evolving* ontologies describe a process rather than a static model. Having protocols for the process of evolving ontologies is the real challenge. Evolving over time is an essential requirement for useful ontologies. As daily practice constantly changes, ontologies that mediate the information needs of these processes must have strong support in *versioning* and must be accompanied by *process models that help to organize consensus.*

Depending on their level of generality, different types of ontologies may be identified that fulfill different roles in the process of building a knowledge-based systems ([Guarino, 1998], [van Heijst et al., 1997]). Among others, we can distinguish the following ontology types:

- *Domain ontologies* capture the knowledge valid for a particular type of domain (e.g. electronic, medical, mechanic, digital domain).

- *Meta data ontologies* like Dublin Core [Weibel et al., 1995] provide a vocabulary for describing the content of on-line information sources.

- *Generic* or *common-sense ontologies* aim at capturing general knowledge about the world, providing basic notions and concepts for things like time, space, state, event, etc. ([Fridman-Noy & Hafner, 1997]). As a consequence, they are valid across several domains. For example, an ontology about mereology (part-of relations) is applicable in many technical domains [Borst & Akkermans, 1997].

- *Representational ontologies* do not commit themselves to any particular domain. Such ontologies provide representational entities without stating what should be represented. A well-known representational ontology is the *Frame-Ontology* [Gruber, 1993], which defines concepts such as frames, slots, and slot constraints allowing the expression of knowledge in an object-oriented or frame-based way.

- Other types of ontology are so-called *method* and *task ontologies* ([Fensel & Groenboom, 1997], [Studer et al., 1996]). Task ontologies provide terms specific for particular tasks (e.g. "hypothesis" belongs to the diagnosis task ontology), and method ontologies provide terms specific to particular problem-solving methods (e.g. "correct state" belongs to the propose-and-revise method ontology). Task and method ontologies provide a reasoning point of view on domain knowledge.

In the following, we will discuss some illustrations: WordNet, Cyc, TOVE, and (KA)^2.

WordNet[1] (see [Fellbaum, 1999]) is an on-line lexical reference system whose design is inspired by current psycho linguistic theories of human lexical memory. English nouns, verbs, adjectives and adverbs are organized into synonym sets, each representing one underlying lexical concept. Different relations link the synonym sets. It was developed by the Cognitive Science Laboratory at Princeton University. WordNet contains around 100,000 word *meanings* organized in a taxonomy. WordNet groups words into five categories: *noun*, *verb*, *adjective*, *adverb*, and *function word*. Within each category it organizes the words by concepts (i.e., word meanings) and semantical relationship between words. Examples of these relationships are:

- *Synonymy*: Similarity in meaning of words, which is used to build concepts represented by a set of words.

- *Antonymy*: Dichotomy in meaning of words, mainly used for organizing adjectives and adverbs.

- *Hyponymy*: Is-a relationship between concepts. This is-a hierarchy ensures the inheritance of properties from super-concepts to sub-concepts.

- *Meronymy*: Part-of relationship between concepts.

- *Morphological*: relations which are used to reduce word forms.

---

[1]   http://www.cogsci.princeton.edu/~wn

The success of WordNet is based on the fact that it is available on-line, free of charge, and that it is a dictionary based on concepts, i.e. it provides much more than just an alphabetic list of words. A multilingual European version EuroWordNet[2] has also come into being. Specific features of WordNet are its large size (i.e., number of concepts), its domain-independence, and its low level of formalization. By the latter I mean that WordNet does not provide any semantic definitions in a formal language. The semantics of concepts is defined with natural language terms. This leaves definitions vague and limits the possibility for automatic reasoning support. WordNet is mainly linguistically motivated. In this respect, WordNet can be seen as one extreme of a spectrum where Cyc defines the other extreme.

Cyc[3] [Lenat & Guha, 1990] was initiated in the course of research into artificial intelligence, making common-sense knowledge accessible and processable for computer programs. The lack of common-sense knowledge and reasoning was encountered in many if not all application areas of artificial intelligence as the main barrier to enabling intelligence. Take machine learning as an example: on the one hand, learning is a prerequisite of intelligence; on the other hand, intelligence is a prerequisite for meaningful learning. Humans decide based on their common-sense knowledge what to learn and what not to learn from their observations. Cyc started as an approach to formalizing this knowledge of the world and providing it with a formal and executable semantics. Hundreds of thousands of concepts have since been formalized with millions of logical axioms, rules, and other assertions which specify constraints on the individual objects and classes. Some of them are publicly available on the Web page. The upper-level ontology of Cyc with 3000 concepts has been made publicly available. These are the most generic concepts which are situated at a high level in the taxonomy of concepts. Most of the more specific concepts are kept secret as property of Cycorp, the company that markets Cyc.

Cyc groups concepts into microtheories to structure the overall ontology. Microtheories are a means to express the context dependency of knowledge (i.e., what is right in one context may be wrong in another one, see [Lenat, submitted]). They are a means to structure the whole knowledge base, which would be otherwise inconsistent and unmaintainable. Each microtheory is a logical theory introducing terms and defining their semantics with logical axioms. CycL, a variant of predicate logic, is used as language for expressing these theories. Like WordNet, Cyc is rather large and domain-independent. In contrast to WordNet it provides formal and operational definitions.

---

[2] http://www.illc.uva.nl/EuroWordNet
[3] http://www.cyc.com

TOVE[4] ([Fox et al., 1993], [Fox & Gruninger, 1997]) is an example of a task- and domain-specific ontology. The ontology supports enterprise integration, providing a sharable representation of knowledge. The goal of the TOVE (TOronto Virtual Enterprise) project is to create a generic, reusable data model that has the following characteristics:

- it provides a shared terminology for the enterprise that each agent can jointly understand and use,

- it defines the meaning of each term as precise and unambiguous as possible,

- it implements the semantics in a set of axioms that will enable TOVE to automatically deduce the answer to many "common-sense" questions about the enterprise, and

- it defines a symbology for depicting a term or the concept constructed thereof in a graphical context.

In consequence, TOVE provides a reusable representation (i.e., ontology) of industrial concepts. Using ontologies for information exchange and business transactions is also investigated in [Uschold et al., 1996].

The *Knowledge Annotation Initiative of the Knowledge Acquisition Community*, known as *(KA)²* (see [Benjamins et al., 1999]), was a case study on:

- the process of developing an ontology for a heterogeneous and world wide (research) community, and

- the use of the ontology for providing semantic access to on-line information sources of this community.

$(KA)^2$ comprises three main subtasks: (1) Ontological engineering to build an ontology of the subject matter; (2) characterizing the knowledge in terms of the ontology; and (3) providing intelligent access to the knowledge. In $(KA)^2$, an ontology of the knowledge acquisition community (see an "enterprise knowledge map") was built. Since an ontology should capture consensual knowledge, several researchers cooperated together – at different locations – to construct the ontology in $(KA)^2$. In this way, it was ensured that the ontology will be accepted by a majority of knowledge acquisition researchers. The design criteria used to build this ontology were: modularity, to allow more flexibility and a variety of uses; specialization of general concepts into more specific concepts; classification of concepts to enable inheritance of common features; and standardized name conventions. The

---

[4] http://www.eil.utoronto.ca/tove/toveont.html

ontology for the KA community consists of seven related ontologies: an organization ontology, a project ontology, a person ontology, a research-topic ontology, a publication ontology, an event ontology, and a research-product ontology. The first six ontologies are rather generic, while the seventh (i.e., the research-topic ontology) is specific to the investigated domain (see Fig. 1). Actually, a meta-ontology (i.e., a template) for describing research topics was defined first. Then this template was instantiated for the research topics. The topics that were identified in a number of international meetings are: reuse; problem-solving methods; ontologies; validation and verification; specification languages; knowledge acquisition methodologies; agent-oriented approaches; knowledge acquisition from natural language; knowledge management; knowledge acquisition through machine learning; knowledge acquisition through Conceptual Graphs; foundations of knowledge acquisition; evaluation of knowledge acquisition techniques and methodologies; and knowledge elicitation. Each of these topics was given to a small group of experts who completed the scheme in Fig. 1.

```
Class: research-topic
Attributes:
   Name: <string>
   Description: <text>
   Approaches: <set-of keyword>
   Research-groups: <set-of research-group>
   Researchers: <set-of researcher>
   Related-topics: <set-of research-topic>
   Subtopics: <set-of research-topic>
   Events: <set-of events>
   Journals: <set-of journal>
   Projects: <set-of project>
   Application-areas: <text>
   Products: <set-of product>
   Bibliographies: <set-of HTML-link>
   Mailing-lists: <set-of mailing-list>
   Webpages: <set-of HTML-link>
   International-funding-agencies: <funding-agency>
   National-funding-agencies: <funding-agency>
   Author-of-Ontology: <set-of researcher>
   Date-of-last-modification: <date>
```

Fig. 1   The meta-ontology for specifying research topics in (KA)[2]

Summary. An ontology provides an explicit conceptualization (i.e., *meta-information*) that describes the semantics of the data. It has a similar function to a database schema. The differences are[5]:

- A language for defining ontologies is syntactically and semantically richer than common approaches for databases.

- The information that is described by an ontology consists of semistructured natural language texts and not tabular information.

- An ontology must be a shared and consensual terminology because it is used for information sharing and exchange.

- An ontology provides a domain theory and not the structure of a data container.

In a nutshell, ontology research is database research for the 21st century where data need to be shared and not always fit into a simple table.

---

[5] See [Meersman, 2000] for an elaborated comparison of database schemes and ontologies.

3   Languages

This chapter is devoted to the language infrastructure that will enable ontologies to be put into practise. We have already mentioned the fact that computers are changing from single isolated devices to entry points into a worldwide network of information exchange and business transactions. Therefore, support for data, information, and knowledge exchange is becoming the key issue in computer technology. In consequence, strenuous efforts are being made towards a new standard for defining and exchanging data structures. The *eXtendible Markup Language (XML)* is a Web standard that provides such facilities. In this chapter we will therefore investigate XML in detail before going on to describe how it relates to the use of ontologies for information exchange. The *Resource Description Framework (RDF)* is a second important standard when talking about the Web and ontologies. Ontologies are formal theories about a certain domain of discourse and therefore require a formal logical language to express them. We will discuss some of the major formal approaches and we will investigate how recent Web standards such as XML and RDF relate to languages that express ontologies.

3.1   XML

XML is a tag-based language for describing tree structures with a linear syntax. It is a successor to the Standard Generalized Markup Language (SGML), which was developed long ago for describing document structures. However, whereas HTML is too simple to serve our purpose, SGML was seen to be too complex to become a widely used standard. XML simplifies some aspects of SGML that were not viewed as essential. An example of a simple XML document is provided in Fig. 2.

XML provides seven different means for presenting information:

1   Elements
    Elements are the typical element of a markup: `<tag>` contents `</tag>`

```
<?XML version="1.0"?>
<homepage>
  <heading>This is Fensel's Homepage!</heading>
  <paragraph>
    Hello! My Name is
    <name>Dieter Fensel</name>
    and my email is:<br/>
    <email>dfe@aifb.uni-karlsruhe.de</email>
    and my phone number is:<br/>
    <phone type="office">6084751</phone>
    <phone type="private">9862155</phone>
  </paragraph>
</homepage>
```

Fig. 2 A simple XML example

2 Attributes

Attributes are name-value pairs defined within a tag

```
<tag attribute-name="attribute-value" ... ></tag>
```

3 References

References can be used to write symbols in a text that would otherwise be interpreted as commands, for example, "<" can be written as < for use as text in XML. References can also be used to define macros. Often-used text or links can be defined as macros and need to be written and maintained only at one place. Entity references always start with "&" and end with ";".

4 Comments

Comments begin with <!-- and end with -->. XML processors could ignore comments.

5 Processing Instructions

Processing Instructions (PI) are the procedural element in an otherwise declarative approach. Processing Instructions have the form:

```
<?name pidata?>
```

An XML processor could ignore Processing Instructions like comments, but must pass them through to the application. The application executes all Processing Instructions it knows. An example for a Processing Instruction is:

```
<?xml:stylesheet type="text/css2" href="style.css" ?>
```

6 CDATA

CDATA represents arbitrary strings in XML Documents which are not interpreted by an XML parser.

```
<![CDATA[
    XML uses <begin-tag> and <end-tag> to structure documents.
]]>
```

7 Prolog

The XML declaration: `<?XML version="1.0"?>` is obligatory. In addition a prolog may contain further elements. An XML document may use a document type declaration either by containing its definition or by pointing to it. Such a document type declaration defines a grammar for XML documents and is called a *Document Type Definition (DTD)*. An external definition which is pointed to by a reference looks like this:

```
<!DOCTYPE Name SYSTEM "name.dtd">
```

while an internal definition looks like

```
<!DOCTYPE Name [<!ELEMENT Name (#PCDATA)>]>
```

3.1.1   What Are DTDs?

In this section we will discuss the usefulness of DTDs and then show how DTDs can be defined. An XML document is *well formed* if

- the document starts with an XML declaration;
- all tags with contents have begin and end tags; tags without contents have an end tag or end with "`/>`";
- it has a root (XML documents are trees).

An XML document is *valid* if it is *well formed*, and if the document uses a DTD it respects this DTD. Therefore, DTDs are not necessary for XML documents; however, they provide the ability to define stronger constraints for documents.

A DTD consists of three elements: an *element* declaration that defines composed tags and value ranges for elementary tags; an *attribute* declaration that define attributes of tags; and an *entity* declaration.

```
<?XML version="1.0"?>
  <!DOCTYPE name [
    <!ELEMENT name (title*, first name | initial, middle name?,
      last name +)>]>
  <!DOCTYPE first name [
    <!ELEMENT first name #PCDATA¹>]>
  <name>
    <title>Privatdozent</title>
    <title>Dr.</title>
    <first name>Dieter</first name>
    <last name>Fensel</last name>
  </name>
```

---

[1] parseable character data

Fig. 3   A simple element declaration

An example of element declarations and a valid XML document is given in Fig. 3. In this the following hold true:

- "?" = zero or one appearance of an element
- "*" = zero to n appearances of an element
- "+" = one to n appearances of an element
- "a | b" = a or b appearances of an element

Attribute declarations regulate the following aspects: the elements that may have an attribute; the attributes they have; the values an attribute may have; and the default value of an attribute. Its general form is:

```
<!ATTLIST element-name
    attribute-name₁ attribute-type₁ default-value₁
    ...
    attribute-nameₙ attribute-typeₙ default-valueₙ
>
```

There are six attribute types: CDATA = string; ID = Unique key; IDREF and IDREFS = reference for one or several IDs in the document; ENTITY or ENTITIES = name of one or several entities; NMTOKEN or NMTOKENS = value is one or several words; and a list of names (enumeration type).

Finally, four types of default values can be distinguished:

- `#REQUIRED`. The attribute must have a value.

- `#IMPLIED`. The attribute must have a value and no default value is defined.

- `"value"`. This value is the value of the attribute if nothing else is defined explicitly.

- `#FIXED "value"`. If the attribute is used it must have this default value.

Entities enable the definition of symbolic values. This may provide shortcuts for long expressions, for example *dfe* for *Privatdozent Dr. Dieter Andreas Fensel*.

```
<!ENTITY dfe "Privatdozent Dr. Dieter Andreas Fensel">
```

Even more important, it significantly improves the maintainability of XML documents. Elements that appear in several places within a document need only be changed once based on their central description.

XML Schema is another means of defining constraints on the syntax and structure of valid XML documents (see [Biron & Malhotra, 2000], [Thompson et al., 2000], [Walsh, 1999]). A more accessible explanation of XML Schema can be found in [Fallside, 2000]. XML schemas have the same purpose as DTDs, but provide several significant improvements:

- XML schema definitions are themselves XML documents.

- XML schema provides a rich set of data types that can be used to define the values of elementary tags.

- XML schema provides a much richer means of defining nested tags (i.e., tags with sub-tags).

- XML schema provides the name-space mechanism to combine XML documents with heterogeneous vocabulary.

Compared to DTDs, XML schema provide various advantages; however, working with them and developing tools for them are more complex.

3.1.2   Linking in XML

HyperText Markup Language (HTML) provides representation of textual information and hyperlinks between various documents and parts hereof. XML incorporates a similar but generalized linking mechanism. In general, three kinds of links will be provided: simple links, extended links, and extended pointers.

Simple links resemble HTML links, for example,

```
<LINK XML-LINK="SIMPLE" HREF="locator">text</LINK>
```

However, the locator may be an URL (as in HTML), a query (see XML-QL), or an extended pointer (see below).

Extended links can express relations with more than two addressees:

```
<ELINK XML-LINK="EXTENDED" ROLE="ANNOTATIONS">
   <LOCATOR XML-LINK="LOCATOR" HREF="text.loc">text
   </LOCATOR>
   <LOCATOR XML-LINK="LOCATOR" HREF="Annot₁.loc">Ann₁
   </LOCATOR>
   <LOCATOR XML-LINK="LOCATOR" HREF="Annot₂.loc">Ann₂
   </LOCATOR>
</ELINK>
```

Extended Pointers (XPointers). In HTML an URL can point to a specific part of a document, for example, "http://www.a.b/c#name" where "name" is the name of an anchor tag. In XML you can jump to an arbitrary location within a document, for example, in a list of employees you can jump to the row of employees with the name *Miller* or to the 10th row or to the row with the ID "007". Therefore, XPointers are similar to general queries.

3.1.3   Extendible Style Language (XSL)

A browser can render an HTML document because it recognizes all HTML tags. Therefore it can use predefined style information. However, in XML tags can be defined by the information provider. How does a browser render XML documents? It requires additional style sheet information for this purpose. *Cascading Stylesheets (CSSs)* define how a browser should render XML documents. It has already been developed for HTML to allow more flexibility in layout, helping to bring HTML back to its original purpose of being a language for describing the structure of documents instead of their layout. A more expressive choice in the case of XML is XSL. This is the upcoming standard for expressing format information of XML documents, but, it can do much more than this. CSS defines for each element of a document how it should be rendered. XSL allows us to define views that manipulate the structure and elements of an document before they are rendered. Therefore, XSL even enables the translation of one XML document into another using a different DTD. This is important in cases where different users may wish to have different *views* of the information captured in an XML document. In electronic commerce applications, it enables different product presentations for different clients and for different user groups (for example, clients who build and maintain product catalogues versus users who access these catalogs). Therefore, XSL has more expressive power than CSS. It is comparable to the expressiveness of DSSSL which is used for presenting SGML documents. However, in contrast to the Lisp syntax of DSSSL, XSL has an XML syntax.

At the moment, XSL can be used for server-site translation of XML documents into HTML. HTML is just another XML dialect and this translation by the server is required because most browsers currently do not support XML and XSL for rendering. In general, the dynamic manipulation of XML documents can be used to create different pages from the same data sources, and to realize dynamically changing pages according to user preferences or contexts. XML is a standard language for defining tagged languages. However, XML does not provide standard DTDs, i.e., each user can/may/must define his own DTD. For exchanging data between different users relying on different DTDs, you have to map different DTDs onto each other. You can use XSL to translate XML documents using DTD_1 into XML documents using DTD_2 providing the translation service required for electronic commerce mentioned earlier. *Precisely here lies the importance of XSL* in our context.

How does XSL achieve this? XSL is a language for expressing style-sheets. Each stylesheet describes rules for presenting a class of XML source documents. There are two parts to the presentation process: First, the result tree is constructed from the source tree. Second, the result tree is interpreted to produce formatted output on a display, on paper, in speech or on other media.

The first part is achieved by *associating patterns with templates*.

* A *pattern* is matched against elements in the source tree.
* A *template* is instantiated to create part of the result tree.
* The result tree is separate from the source tree.

In consequence, the structure of the result tree can be completely different from the structure of the source tree. In constructing the result tree, the source tree can be filtered and reordered, and arbitrary structure can be added.

The second part, formatting, is achieved by using the formatting vocabulary specified in this document to construct the result tree.

The following is an example of a simple XSL stylesheet that constructs a result tree for a sequence of paraelements. The result-ns="fo" attribute indicates that a tree using the formatting object vocabulary is being constructed. The rule for the root node specifies the use of a page sequence formatted with any font with serifs. The paraelements become block formatting objects which are set in 10 point type with a 12 point space before each block.

```
<xsl:stylesheet>
   xmlns:xsl="http://www.w3.org/TR/WD-xsl"
   xmlns:fo="http://www.w3.org/TR/WD-xsl/FO"
   result-ns="fo">
   <xsl:template match="/">
      <fo:basic-page-sequence font-family="serif">
         <xsl:apply-templates/>
      </fo:basic-page-sequence>
   </xsl:template>
   <xsl:template match="para">
      <fo:block font-size="10pt" space-before="12pt">
         <xsl:apply-templates/>
      </fo:block>
   </xsl:template>
</xsl:stylesheet>
```

Fig. 4 A simple XSL document

- Formally, this vocabulary is an XML name space. Each element type in the vocabulary corresponds to a formatting object class.

- A formatting object class represents a particular kind of formatting behavior.

- Each attribute in the vocabulary corresponds to a formatting property.

- A formatting object can have content, and its formatting behavior is applied to its content.

An example of an XSL file is provided in Fig. 4.

3.1.4   Additional Information

There are large quantities of information available about XML. The official Web pages about XML are hosted by the W3C,[1] the standardization committee of the World Wide Web.

---

[1] http://www.w3c.org

In addition, there is an excellent FAQ list at http://www.ucc.ie/xml and numerous books dealing with XML have appeared (e.g., [Connolly, 1997]). Articles and tutorials on XML can be found at:

- http://metalab.unc.edu/pub/sun-info/standards/xml/why/xmlapps.html
- http://www.inrialpes.fr/inria/seminaires/XML1-10.12.98/sld00000.htm
- http://www.inrialpes.fr/inria/seminaires/XML2-10.12.98/sld00000.htm
- http://www.gca.org/conf/paris98/bosak/sld00000.htm
- http://www.heise.de/ix/raven/Web/xml

Finally, Robin Covers' site at OASIS is one of the richest online sources on these topics: http://www.oasis-open.org/cover/xml.html.

3.2   RDF

XML provides semantic information as a by-product of defining the structure of the document. It prescribes a tree structure for documents and the different leaves of the tree have well-defined tags and contexts with which the information can be understood. That is, the structure and semantics of documents are interwoven. The *Resource Description Framework*[2] (see [Miller, 1998], [Lassila & Swick, 1999]) provides a means of adding semantics to a document without making any assumptions about its structure. RDF is an infrastructure that enables the encoding, exchange, and reuse of structured metadata. Search engines, intelligent agents, information brokers, browsers and human users can make use of *semantic* information. RDF is an XML application (i.e., its syntax is defined in XML) customized for adding meta-information to Web documents and will be used by other standards such as PICS-2, P3P, and DigSig (see Fig. 5).

The RDF data model provides three object types: *subjects*, *predicates*, and *objects* (see the schema definition of RDF [Brickley et al., 1998]).

- A *subject* is an entity that can be referred to by an address on the WWW (i.e., by an URL or URI). Resources are the elements that are described by RDF statements.
- An *predicate* defines a binary relation between resources and/or atomic values provided by primitive data type definitions in XML.
- An *object* specifies a value for a subject's predicate. That is, objects provide the actual characterizations of the Web documents.

---

[2]   http://www.w3c.org/Metadata

A simple example is[3]

```
Author(http://www.cs.vu.nl/frankh) = Frank
```

This states that the author of the named Web document is Frank. Values can also be structured entities:

```
Author(http://www.cs.vu.nl/frankh) = X
Name(X) = Frank
Email(X) = frankh@cs.vu.nl
```

where X denotes an actual (i.e., the homepage of Frank) or a virtual URI. In addition, RDF provides bags, sequence, and alternatives to express collections of Web sources.

Finally, RDF can be used to make statements about RDF statements, i.e. it provides meta-level facilities:

```
Claim(Dieter)=(Author(http://www.cs.vu.nl/frankh) = Frank)
```

states that *Dieter* claims that *Frank* is the author of the named resource.

RDF schemes (RDFS) [Brickley et al., 1998] provide a basic type schema for RDF based on core classes, core property types and core constraints.

Three core classes are provided by the RDF Schema machinery:

- *Resource* (i.e., the class of all subjects);
- *Property Type* (i.e., the class of all predicates); and
- *Class* (i.e., the class of all values of predicates).

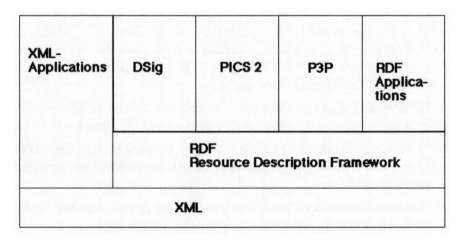

Fig. 5   The Resource Description Framework

---

[3] I will skip the awkward syntax of RDF, because simple tooling can easily present it in a more common format such as shown here.

Core property types of RDFS are:

- *instanceOf* and *subClassOf*: *instanceOf* defines a relationship between a *resource* and an element of *Class,* and *subClassOf* defines a relationship between two elements of *Class*. *subClassOf* is assumed to be transitive.

- *Constraint* is a subclass of *PropertyType*. It has the two core instances *range* and *domain* applicable to property types having a class as value. *Range* and *domain* define the range and domain of property types respectively.

XML, XSL, and RDF are complementary technological means that will enable ontological support in knowledge management and electronic commerce. XML provides a standard serial syntax for exchanging data. In consequence, ontology-based data and information exchange can abstract from these aspects. A DTD allows us to define the structure and elementary tags of an XML document. We will see later how such a DTD can be generated from an ontology and vice versa. XSL allows us to translate between different XML documents, i.e., documents relying on different DTDs. Finally, RDF provides a standard for describing machine-processable semantics of data. The relationships between new and forthcoming Web standards on the one hand and ontology languages on the other hand will be discussed later.

3.3   Ontology Languages

We will discuss some ontology languages that are well known in the community and that are prototypical of a specific language paradigm. These are:

- CycL and KIF [Genesereth, 1991] as representatives of enriched first-order predicate logic languages.

- Ontolingua [Farquhar et al., 1997] and Frame Logic [Kifer et al., 1995] as representatives of frame-based approaches. Both in-corporate frame-based modeling primitives in a first-order logical framework, but they apply very different strategies for this.

- Description logics that describe knowledge in terms of concepts and role restrictions used to automatically derive classification taxonomies.

3.3.1   Predicate Logic Languages CycL And KIF

CycL was developed in the Cyc project [Lenat & Guha, 1990] for the purpose of specifying the large common-sense ontology that should provide artificial intelligence to computers. Far from having attained this goal, Cyc still provides the world's largest formalized ontology. CycL is a formal language whose syntax is derived from first-order predicate calculus. However, CycL extends first-order logic through the use of *second*-order concepts. Predicates are also treated as constants in expressions. The vocabulary of CycL consists of terms: semantic constants, non-atomic terms, variables, numbers, strings, etc. Terms are combined in CycL expressions, ultimately forming closed CycL sentences (with no free variables). A set of CycL sentences forms a knowledge base. In the following, we will discuss the main concepts of CycL. More details can be found on its homepage.[4]

Constants are the vocabulary of the CycL language; more precisely, they are the "words" that are used in writing the axioms (i.e., the closed formulas) that comprise the content of any CycL knowledge base. Constants may denote (1) individuals, (2) collections of other concepts (i.e., sets which correspond to unary predicates), or (3) arbitrary predicates that enable the expression of relationships among other constants and functions. Constants must have unique names.

Predicates express relationships between terms. The *type* of each argument of each predicate must be specified; that is, the appropriate formulas must be asserted to be true, i.e. $p(A_0)$ with A_0 of type T and $p(c)$ implies that c is an element of T.

Variables stand for terms (e.g., constants) or formulas whose identities are not specified. A variable may appear anywhere that a term or formula can appear.

Formulas combine terms into meaningful expressions. Each formula has the structure of a parenthesized list. That is, it starts with a left parenthesis, then it follows a series of objects which are commonly designated A_0, A_1, A_2, etc., and at the end there is a corresponding right parenthesis. The object in the A_0 position may be a predicate, a logical connective, or a quantifier. The remaining arguments may be terms (e.g., constants, non-atomic terms, variables, numbers, strings delimited by double quotes ("...")), or other formulas. Note the recursion (i.e., the second-order syntax) here; A_i in one formula might itself be an entire CycL formula. Each atomic formula must begin with a predicate or a variable in order to be wellformed. The simplest

---

[4] http://www.cyc.com/cycl.html

kind of formula is in which the A_0 position is occupied by a predicate and all the other argument positions are filled with terms (or variables):

```
(likesAsFriend DougLenat KeithGoolsbey)
(colorOfObject ?CAR ?COLOR)
```

The first formula above is called a ground atomic formula, since none of the terms filling the argument positions are variables. The second formula is not a ground atomic formula; it refers to the variables ?CAR and ?COLOR.

Logical connectives are used to build more complex formulas from atomic formulas (and/or other complex formulas). The most important logical connectives are *and*, *or*, and *not*. New connectives can be introduced simply by inserting a formula to that effect into the knowledge base; thus

```
(isa new-connector Connective).
```

Complex Formulas. We can compose the above connectives, of course, and have complex expressions such as

```
(and ... (or ... (xor A (and ... ))...)...)
```

Quantification comes in two main flavors: universal quantification and existential quantification. Universal quantification corresponds to expressions like *every*, *all*, *always*, *everyone*, and *anything*, while existential quantification corresponds to expressions like someone, something, and somewhere. CycL contains **one universal quantifier**, *forAll*, and **four existential quantifiers** *thereExists*, *thereExistAtLeast*, *thereExistAtMost*, and *thereExistExactly*. Additional quantifiers can be introduced by making the appropriate assertions – declaring the new quantifier to be an instance of Quantifier, and giving a definition of it, probably in terms of existing quantifiers, predicates, and collections. To be considered a closed sentence – a well-formed formula – all the variables in an expression need to be *bound* by a quantifier before they are used.

Second-order Quantification. Quantification is also allowed over predicates, functions, arguments, and formulas.

Functions. Like most predicates, most functions have a fixed arity. For each function assertions that specify the type of each argument must be entered into the CycL knowledge base.

Microtheories ([Lenat & Guha, 1990], [Guha, 1993]). A microtheory, or context ([McCarthy 1993], [Lenat, submitted]), is a set of formulas in the knowledge base. Each formula must be asserted in at least one micro-theory. Microtheories are fully reified objects, and thus they can not only contain CycL formulas, but also participate in CycL formulas.

Each formula has an associated **truth value** (in each microtheory). CycL contains five possible non-numeric truth values, of which the most common are default true and monotonically true. The other truth values are default false, monotonically false, and unknown. In addition, CycL accommodates Bayesian probabilities and dependencies, and (separately) fuzzy truth values, attributes, and sets. All CycL-compliant systems must support at least one "true" and one "false" value.

- **Monotonically true** means true with no exceptions. Assertions which are monotonically true are held to be true in every case, that is, for every possible set of bindings – not just currently known bindings – to the universally quantified variables (if any) in the assertion and cannot be overridden.

- Assertions which are **default true**, in contrast to monotonically true, can have exceptions. They are held to be true only in most cases (usually meaning most of the relevant cases likely to be encountered in the current context) and can be overridden without needing to alert the user.

In a nutshell, CycL uses predicate logic extended by *typing* (i.e. functions and predicates are typed), *reification* (i.e. predicates and formulas are treated as terms and can be used as expressions within other formulas), and microtheories that define a *context* for the truth of formulas.

The *Knowledge Interchange Format (KIF)* [Genesereth & Fikes, 1992] is a language designed for use in the exchange of knowledge between disparate computer systems (created by different programmers at different time, in different languages, etc.). Different computer systems can interact with their users in whatever forms are most appropriate to their applications. Being a language for knowledge interchange, KIF can also be used as a language for expressing and exchanging ontologies.[5] The following categorical features are essential to the design of KIF.

- The language has *declarative semantics*.

- The language is *logically comprehensive*-at its most general it provides for the expression of arbitrary logical sentences. In this way, it differs

---

[5] Actually, KIF was not presented in this way because its origins are older than the current O-hip.

from relational database languages (like SQL) and logic programming languages (like Prolog).

- The language provides a *means for the representation of knowledge about knowledge*. This allows the user to make knowledge representation decisions explicit and to introduce new knowledge representation constructs without changing the language.

Semantically, there are four categories of **constants** in KIF-object constants, function constants, relation constants, and logical constants. Object constants are used to denote individual objects. Function constants denote functions on those objects. Relation constants denote relations. Logical constants express conditions about the world and are either true or false. KIF is unusual among logical languages in that there is no syntactic distinction between these four types of constants; any constant can be used where any other constant can be used. The differences between these categories of constants are entirely semantic. This feature *reifies* second-order features in KIF. It is possible to make statements about statements.

There are three disjoint types of **expressions** in the language: *terms*, *sentences*, and *definitions*. Terms are used to denote objects in the world being described, sentences are used to express facts about the world, and definitions are used to define constants. A *knowledge base* is a finite set of sentences and definitions.

There are six types of **sentences**.

```
sentence ::= constant | equation | inequality | relsent |
    logsent | quantsent
```

We have already mentioned constants. An equation consists of the "=" operator and two terms. An inequality consist of the "/=" operator and two terms. An implicit relational sentence consists of a constant and an arbitrary number of argument terms terminated by an optional sequence variable.

The syntax of **logical sentences** depends on the logical operator involved. A sentence involving the *not* operator is called a negation. A sentence involving the *and* operator is called a conjunction and the arguments are called conjuncts. A sentence involving the *or* operator is called a disjunction and the arguments are called disjuncts. A sentence involving the "=>" operator is called an implication; all of its arguments but the last are called antecedents and the last argument is called the consequent. A sentence involving the "<=" operator is called a reverse implication; its first argument is called the consequent and the remaining arguments are called the antecedents. A sentence involving the "<=>" operator is called an equivalence.

There are two types of **quantified sentences** – a universally quantified sentence is signaled by the use of the forall operator, and an existentially quantified sentence is signaled by the use of the exists operator. The first argument in each case is a list of variable specifications. Note that according to these rules it is permissible to write sentences with *free* variables,[6] i.e. variables that do not occur within the scope of any enclosing quantifier.

Finally, there are three types of **definitions** – unrestricted, complete, and partial. Within each type there are four cases, one for each category of constant. For more details see the KIF homepage.[7]

KIF and CycL have features in common. Both languages are oriented on predicate logics. Also, both provide an important extension of first-order logic. They allow the reification of formulas as terms used in other formulas. Therefore, KIF and CycL allow meta-level statements. In addition to this, CycL provides richer modeling primitives than KIF (e.g., various quantifiers and microtheories). This stems from the fact that CycL is a modeling language for ontologies whereas KIF was designed as an exchange format for ontologies. As I will discuss later, both languages are close in spirit to RDF. Second-order elements (i.e., formulas as terms in meta-level formulas) and global scope of properties (i.e., predicates) are common features.

3.3.2   Frame-based Approaches: Ontolingua and Frame Logic

The central modeling primitive of predicate logic are predicates. *Frame-based* and *object-oriented* approaches take a different point of view. Their central modeling primitive are classes (i.e., frames) with certain properties called attributes. These attributes do not have a global scope but are only applicable to the classes which they are defined for (they are typed), and the "same" attribute (i.e., the same attribute name) may be associated with different range and value restrictions when defined for different classes. In the following, we will discuss two frame-oriented approaches: Ontolingua (see [Gruber, 1993], [Farquhar et al., 1997]) and Frame Logic [Kifer et al., 1995].

Ontolingua[8] was designed to support the design and specification of ontologies with a clear logical semantics based on KIF. Ontolingua extends KIF using additional syntax to include the intuitive bundling of axioms into definitional forms with ontological significance and a frame ontology to

---

[6] Very different from CycL, where free variables are forbidden.
[7] http://logic.stanford.edu/kif/kif.html
[8] http://ontolingua.stanford.edu

define object-oriented and frame-language terms.[9] The Frame-Ontology defines the set of KIF expressions that Ontolingua allows. This specifies the representation primitives that are often supported by special-purpose syntax and code in object-centered representation systems (e.g., classes, instances, slot constraints). Ontolingua definitions are Lisp-style forms that associate a symbol with an argument list, a documentation string, and a set of KIF sentences labeled by keywords. An Ontolingua ontology is made up of definitions of classes, relations, functions, distinguished objects, and axioms that relate these terms.

A **relation** is defined with a form like the following:

```
(define-relation name (?A₁ ?A₂)
:def (KIF formula)
```

The arguments $?A_1$ and $?A_2$ are universally quantified variables ranging over the items in the tuples of the relation. This example is a binary relation, so each tuple in the relation has two items. Relations of greater arity can also be defined. The sentence after the :def keyword is a KIF sentence stating logical constraints over the arguments. Constraints on the value of the first argument of a binary relation are domain restrictions, and those on the second argument of a binary relation are range restrictions. There may also be complex expressions stating relationships among the arguments of the relation. The :def constraints are necessary conditions, which must hold if the relation holds over some arguments. It is also possible to state sufficient conditions or any combination.

A **class** is defined by a similar form with exactly one argument called the instance variable. In Ontolingua, classes are treated as unary relations to help unify object- and relation-centered representation styles.

A **function** is defined like a relation. A slight variation in syntax moves the final argument outside of the argument list. As in definitions of relations, the arguments to a function are constrained with necessary conditions following the :def keyword.

Finally, it is possible to define **individuals** in an ontology.

The Frame-Ontology is expressed as second-order axioms in Ontolingua. It contains a complete axiomatization of classes and instances, slots and slot constraints, class and relation specialization, relation inverses, relation composition, and class partitions. Each second-order term is defined with KIF axioms. A list of the Frame-Ontology vocabulary is given in Figure 6.

---

[9] The Ontolingua server as described in [Farquhar et al., 1997] has extended the original language by providing explicit support for building ontological modules that can be assembled, extended, and refined in a new ontology.

```
class relation (?relation)
class function (?function)
class class (?class)
relation instance-of (?individual ?class)
function all-instances (?class) :->
    ?set-of-instances
function one-of (@instances) :-> ?class
relation subclass-of (?child-class ?parent-class)
relation superclass-of (?parent-class ?child-
class)
relation subrelation-of
    (?child-relation ?parent-relation)
relation direct-instance-of (?individual ?class)
relation direct-subclass-of
    (?child-class ?parent-class)
function arity (?relation) :-> ?n
function exact-domain (?relation) :->
    ?domain-relation
function exact-range (?relation) :-> ?class
relation total-on (?relation ?domain-relation)
relation onto (?relation ?range-class)
class n-ary-relation (?relation)
class unary-relation (?relation)
class binary-relation (?relation)
class unary-function (?function)
relation single-valued (?binary-relation)
function inverse (?binary-relation) :-> ?relation
function projection (?relation ?column) :-> ?class
function composition
    (?relation-1 ?relation-2) :-> ?binary-rela-
tion
relation composition-of
    (?binary-relation ?list-of-relations)
function compose
    @binary-relations) :-> ?binary-relation
relation alias (?relation-1 ?relation-2)
relation domain (?relation ?class)
relation domain-of
    (?domain-class ?binary-relation)
relation range (?relation ?class)
relation range-of (?class ?relation)
relation nth-domain
    (?relation ?integer ?domain-class)
relation has-value
    (?domain-instance ?binary-relation ?value)
function all-values (?domain-instance
    ?binary-relation) :-> ?set-of-values
```

```
relation value-type
    (?domain-instance ?binary-relation ?class)
function value-cardinality
    (?domain-instance ?binary-relation) :-> ?n
relation same-values
    (?domain-instance ?relation-1 ?relation-2)
relation inherited-slot-value
    (?domain-class ?binary-relation ?value)
function all-inherited-slot-values
    (?domain-class ?binary-relation) :-> ?set-of-
    values
relation slot-value-type (?domain-class
    ?binary-relation ?range-class)
function slot-cardinality
    (?domain-class ?binary-relation) :-> ?n
relation minimum-slot-cardinality
    (?domain-class ?binary-relation ?n)
relation maximum-slot-cardinality
    (?domain-class ?binary-relation ?n)
relation single-valued-slot
    (?domain-class ?binary-relation)
relation same-slot-values
    (?domain-class ?relation-1 ?relation-2)
class class-partition (?set-of-classes)
relation subclass-partition (?c ?class-partition)
relation exhaustive-subclass-partition
    (?c ?class-partition)
relation asymmetric-relation (?binary-relation)
relation antisymmetric-relation
    (?binary-relation)
relation antireflexive-relation (?binary-rela-
tion)
relation irreflexive-relation (?binary-relation)
relation reflexive-relation (?binary-relation)
relation symmetric-relation (?binary-relation)
relation transitive-relation (?binary-relation)
relation weak-transitive-relation
    (?binary-relation)
relation one-to-one-relation (?binary-relation)
relation many-to-one-relation (?binary-relation)
relation one-to-many-relation (?binary-relation)
relation many-to-many-relation
    (?binary-relation)
relation equivalence-relation (?binary-relation)
relation partial-order-relation (?binary-rela-
tion)
relation total-order-relation (?binary-relation)
relation documentation (?object ?string)
```

Fig. 6   The Frame-Ontology of Ontolingua (see [Gruber, 1993])

Frame Logic [Kifer et al., 1995] is a language for specifying object-oriented databases, frame systems, and logical programs. Its main achievement is to integrate conceptual modeling constructs (classes, attributes, domain and range restrictions, inheritance, axioms) into a coherent logical framework. Basically it provides classes, attributes with domain and range definitions, is-a hierarchies with set inclusion of subclasses and multiple attribute inheritance, and logical axioms that can be used to further characterize the relationships between elements of an ontology and its instances.

The alphabet of an F-logic language consists of a set of function symbols and a set of variables. A term is a normal first-order term composed of function symbols and variables, as in predicate calculus. A language in F-logic consists of a set of formulas constructed from the alphabet symbols. As in many other logics, formulas are built from simpler formulas by using the usual connectives *not*, *and*, and *or* and the quantifiers *forall* and *exists*. The simplest kind of formulas are called molecular F-formulas. A molecule in F-logic is one of the following statements:

- Assertion of the form C :: D or of the form O : C, where C, D, and O are terms. The first expression models subclass relationship and the second statement models is-element-of relationship.

- An object molecule of the form

    O[a ";"-separated list of method expressions].

    A method expression can be either a data expression or a signature expression. O is a term denoting an object (which may refer to an instance or a class). "a" further specifies properties of this object.

  - A data expression can have one of the following two forms:
    scalar expression

        ScalarMethod @Q_1, ..., Q_k -> T

    set–valued expression

        SetMethod @ R_1, ..., R_1 ->> {S_1, ..., S_m}

    Data expressions specify that the method m applied to the object O and the parameters Q_1,...,Q_k return the value T. They can be either single-valued or may return a set.

  - A signature expression can also take two forms:
    scalar signature expression

        ScalarMethod @V_1, ..., V_n => (A_1, ..., A_r)

    set-valued signature expression

        SetMethod @ W_1, ..., W_s =>> (B_1, ..., B_t)

    Signature expressions define types for applying methods (i.e., attributes) to objects. A method m applied to the object O and the parameter V_1,...,V_m must return a value that is an element/subclass of A_1,...,A_r.

F-formulae are built of simpler F-formulae in the usual manner by means of logical connectives and quantifiers.

Ontolingua and Frame Logic integrate frames (i.e., classes) into a logical framework. The main difference between Ontolingua and Frame Logic is the manner in which they realize frame-based modeling primitives in a logical language. Ontolingua characterizes the frame-based modeling primitives via axioms in the language. Frame Logic defines their semantics externally via an explicit definition of their semantics. To put it simply, Ontolingua applies standard semantics of predicate logic and uses axioms in this logic to exclude models that do not fit the semantics of its modeling primitives. Frame Logic provides a more complex semantics compared to predicate logic. The modeling primitives are explicitly defined in the semantics of Frame Logic. A second difference between Frame Logic and Ontolingua arises from the fact that Ontolingua inherits the powerful reification mechanism from KIF which allows the use of formulas as terms of (meta-level) formulas. In Frame Logic, predicate names can be bound to variables but not entire formulas.

3.3.3   Description Logics

The main thrust of research in knowledge representation is directed at providing theories and systems for expressing structured knowledge and for accessing and reasoning with it in a principled way. *Description logics* (see [Brachman & Schmolze, 1985], [Baader et al., 1991]), also known as *terminological logics*, form an important powerful class of logic-based knowledge representation languages.[10] They stem from early work in semantic networks and define a formal and operational semantics for them. Description Logics try to find a fragment of first-order logic with high expressive power which still has a decidable and efficient inference procedure (see [Muslea et al., 1998]). Systems implemented include BACK, CLASSIC, CRACK, FLEX, K-REP, KL-ONE, KRIS, LOOM, and YAK.[11]

A distinguishing feature of description logics is that classes (usually called concepts) can be defined intensionally in terms of descriptions that specify the properties that objects must satisfy in order to belong to the concept. These descriptions are expressed using a language that allows the construction of composite descriptions, including restrictions on the binary relationships (usually called roles) connecting objects.

Figure 7 provides the syntax definition of the core language of CLASSIC. Its main modeling primitives are concept expressions and individual expressions (see [Borgida et al., 1989]). A CLASSIC database is for the most part a repository of information about individual objects. Objects have an intrinsic identity and are related to each other through binary relationships; these are called *roles* (elsewhere known as attributes or properties). Individuals will be grouped into collections indirectly by means of descriptions that apply to all members of a collection. We will call these descriptions concepts or classes. The data definition language allows the definition of concepts either by grouping individuals together extensionally, or grouping individuals implicitly through the use of intensional descriptions in regard to their structure. Complex CLASSIC concepts are formed by composing expressions using a small set of constructors.

---

[10] Links to most papers, projects, and research events in this area can be found at http://dl.kr.org.
[11] http://www.research.att.com/sw/tools/classic/imp–systems.html

The simplest kind of description you can form in CLASSIC is a **primitive concept**. Primitive concepts are simple but not necessarily atomic; each primitive concept, except for the topmost one (which we call THING), is expected to have at least one parent (more general) concept. The simplest kind of primitive is one whose only parent is essentially vacuous, namely THING. For example, the concept of a CAR might be defined in this way:

(PRIMITIVE THING car) [12]

This expression means that whatever it designates is simply a type of THING with some unspecified difference from THING in general. This is quite the opposite of the case with other (non-primitive) concepts, as we shall see in a moment.

```
<concept-expr> ::=
   THING | CLASSIC-THING | HOST-THING |
   [these three are built-in primitives]
   <concept-name> |
   ( AND <concept-expr> +) [1] |
   ( ALL <role-expr> <concept-expr>) |
   ( AT-LEAST <positive-integer> <role-expr>) |
   ( AT-MOST <non-negative-integer><role-expr>) |
   ( SAME-AS (<role-expr> +) (<role-expr>+)) |
   ( TEST <fn> <realm>) |
   ( ONE-OF <individual-name>+) |
   ( PRIMITIVE <concept-expr> <index>) |
   ( DISJOINT-PRIMITIVE
      <concept-expr> <partition-index> <index>)
<individual-expr> ::=
   <concept-expr> |
   ( FILLS <role-expr> <individual-name>) |
   ( CLOSE <role-expr>) |
   ( AND <individual-expr>+)
<realm> ::= host | classic
<concept-name> ::= <symbol>
<individual-name> ::= <symbol> | <host-lang-expr>
<role-expr> ::= <symbol>
<index> ::= <number> | <symbol>
<partition-index> ::= <number> | <symbol>
<fn> ::= a unary function with boolean return type that can be
evaluated in the host language.
```

---

[1] "+" means one or more values separated by blanks.

Fig. 7   The grammar of the CLASSIC language (taken from [Borgida et al., 1989])

---

[12] This example is taken from [Borgida et al., 1989].

Primitives can also have non-trivial parents. Thus, SPORTS-CAR might be defined as a subconcept of both CAR and another concept, EXPENSIVE-THING:

```
(PRIMITIVE (AND CAR EXPENSIVE-THING)
sports-car).
```

In fact, the parent of a primitive concept can be any CLASSIC concept, including another primitive. Primitives thus specify *necessary* conditions: if *Corvette*$_1$ is an instance of SPORTS-CAR, then it is both a CAR and an EXPENSIVE-THING. But note that there is no sufficiency condition specified for primitive concepts.

The CLASSIC language of concepts allows us to go substantially beyond the simple is-a hierarchies of more traditional semantic data models. It offers three special ways of describing objects in terms of their structure. As we shall see, these constructors allow some class membership relations be determined by inference. CLASSIC's three complex constructors are role *value restrictions*, *cardinality bounds*, and *co-reference constraints*. Role value restrictions are type constraints that hold for the fillers for some single role.

Value restriction. For example, the concept expression

```
(ALL thing-driven CAR)
```

describes any object that is related by the thing-driven role solely to individuals describable by the concept CAR.

Bounds restrict the number of fillers for roles. For example,

```
(AT-MOST 4 thing-driven)
```

describes any object that is related to at most 4 distinct individuals through the thing-driven role, while

```
(AT-LEAST 3 wheel)
```

describes any object that is related to at least 3 distinct individuals through the wheel role.

Co–reference constraints specify simple equalities between single-valued roles or, more generally, chains of such roles. For example, the expression

```
(SAME-AS (driver) (insurance payer))
```

describes all those individuals whose filler for the driver role is the same as for the insurance payer role.

Each of the constructors acts as part of both necessary and sufficient conditions for concepts in which they appear (as long as they are not used in a primitive concept, in which case there are no sufficient conditions).

It is important to note that the meaning of concepts in CLASSIC is determined by their structure. This implies that certain relationships exist between concepts by virtue of their definition. For example, it is quite possible for several different concept expressions to denote the same class:

```
(AND (ALL thing-driven CAR)
(ALL thing-driven EXPENSIVE-THING))
```

is the same concept as

```
(ALL thing-driven
(AND CAR EXPENSIVE-THING)),
```

Various studies have examined extensions of the expressive power of such a language and the trade-off in computational complexity for deriving is-a relationships between concepts and individuals in such a logic. Efficient implementations for core sets of primitives in these languages have been developed (see [Borgida & Patel-Schneider, 1994], [MacGregor, 1994], and [Horrocks & Patel-Schneider, 1999]); see, for example DLP[13] and the FaCT system.[14]

3.4   XML, RDF, and Ontology Languages

In this section we will examine how XML and RDF can be used to express ontologies.

3.4.1   DTD and Ontologies

On the one hand, ontologies and DTD/XML schemes serve very different purposes. Ontology languages are a means to specify domain theories and XML schemes are a means to provide integrity constraints for information sources (i.e., documents and/or semi-structured data). It is therefore not surprising to encounter differences when comparing XML schema with ontology languages. On the other hand, XML Schema and ontology languages have one main goal in common: both provide vocabulary and structure for describing information sources that are aimed at exchange. It is therefore legitimate to compare both and investigate their commonalities and differences. DTD and XML schema definitions define the legal nestings of tags and introduce attributes for them. Defining tags, their nesting, and

---

[13] http://www.bell-labs.com/user/pfps
[14] http://www.cs.man.ac.uk/~horrocks/software.html

attributes for tags may be seen as defining an ontology. However, there are significant differences between an ontology and a DTD.

- First, a DTD specifies the legal *lexical* nesting in a document, which may or may not coincide with an *ontological* hierarchy (subclass relationship). That is, there is nothing in a DTD that corresponds to the is-a relationship of classes that is usually central in an ontology.

- Second, and in consequence, DTDs lack any notion of inheritance. In an ontology, subclasses inherit attributes defined for their super-classes and superclasses inherit instances defined for their subclasses. These inheritance mechanisms do not exist for DTDs.

- Third, DTDs provide a rather poor means for defining the semantics of elementary tags. Basically, a tag can be defined as being composed of other tags or being a string. Usually, ontologies provide a much richer typing concept for describing elementary types.

- Fourth, DTDs define the order in which tags appear in a document. For ontologies, in contrast, the ordering of attribute descriptions does not matter.

We will use an example to clarify these differences (see Fig. 8).

- Concept c_1 has two attributes, a_1 and a_2. This implies that the domains of a_1 and a_2 are the elements of c_1. The range of a_1 is the intersection of c_2 and c_3 and the range of a_2 is the union of c_4 and c_5.

- c_2 is defined as a subclass of c_1. This implies that all attributes defined for c_1 are also applicable for c_2. In addition, each element of c_2 is also an element of c_1.

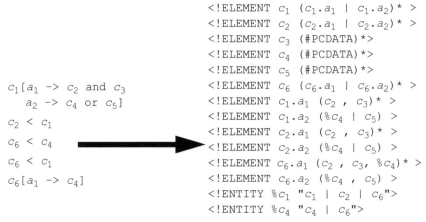

Fig. 8   Translation from an ontology into a DTD

- Finally c_6 is a subclass of c_4 and c_1. Therefore it inherits the attributes a_1 and a_2 from c_1. In addition, it refines the range restriction of attribute a_1 to c_2 and c_3 and c_4. That is, the value of a_1 applied to an element of c_6 must also be an element of c_4. This is not necessary for an element of c_1 that is not also an element of c_6.

When translating this ontology into a DTD we first define c_1 as an element having two sub tags $c_1.a_1$ and $c_1.a_2$, i.e.,

```
<c₁>
    <c₁.a₁> ... </c₁.a₁>
    <c₁.a₂> ... </c₁.a₂>
</c₁>
```

would be a valid document. Therefore, we reify the attribute names with the concept names to distinguish different appearances of attributes in various concepts. A number of problems arise in this translation process:

- The sequence of attribute values of an object does not matter in an ontology, i.e. $o[a_1=5, a_2=3]$ and $o[a_2=3, a_1=5]$ are equivalent. We express this by $(a_1 \mid a_2)^*$. However, this implies that an object may have several values for the same attribute (which is allowed for set-valued but not for single-valued attributes).

- The attribute a_1 has for c_1 as range the intersection of c_2 and c_3. That is, a value of the attribute is an object for which the attributes of c_2 and c_3 can be applied. We express this via $(c_2 , c_3)^*$ which again implies that an object may have several values for the same attribute.

- The only primitive data type is PCDATA, i.e. arbitrary strings.

We can also see the two aspects of inheritance in the translation process.

- First, we have to add all inherited attributes and their inherited range restrictions explicitly. For example:

```
<!ENTITY %c₁ "c₁ | c₂ | c₆">
```

- Second, the value of an attribute may also be the element of a subclass of its value type (i.e., a superclass inherits all elements of its subclasses). Therefore, whenever a class is used as a range restriction we have to add all its subclasses. For this we use the entity mechanism of DTDs. For example:

```
<!ENTITY %c₁ "c₁ | c₂ | c₆">
```

More details and further aspects of ontology to DTD translations can be found in [Erdmann & Studer, 1999] and [Rabarijoana et al., 1999]. In a nutshell, DTDs are rather weak in regard to what can be expressed with them.

Work on *XML schemes* (see [Malhotra & Maloney, 1999]) may well contribute to bridging the gap between DTDs and ontologies. Schemes introduce mechanisms for constraining document structure and content, mechanisms to enable inheritance for element, attribute, and data type definitions, mechanisms for application-specific constraints and descriptions, mechanisms to enable the integration of structural schemes with primitive data types, primitive data typing, including byte, date, integer, sequence, etc., and they allow the creation of user-defined data types. A detailed comparison of XML schemes and ontologies can be found in [Klein et al., 2003]. We will discuss only one quite interesting aspect that is related to the different treatment of inheritance in XML schema and in an ontology.

XML Schema incorporates the notion of type derivation. However, this can only partially be compared with what is provided with inheritance in ontology languages. First, in XML Schema all inheritance has to be modeled explicitly. In ontologies, inheritance can be derived from the definitions of the concepts. Second, XML Schema does not provide a direct way to inherit from multiple parents. Types can only be derived from one base type. Most ontology languages provide multiple inheritance. Third, and very important, the is-a relationship has a twofold role in conceptual modeling which is not directly covered by XML Schema:

- *Top-down inheritance of attributes* from superclasses to subclasses. Assume employee as a subclass of a class person. Then employee inherits all attributes that are defined for person.

- *Bottom-up inheritance of instances* from subclasses to superclasses. Assume employee as a subclass of a class person. Then person inherits all instances (i.e., elements) that are an element of employee.

In XML Schema, both aspects can only be modeled in an artificial way. The top-down inheritance of attributes is difficult to model, because type derivations in XML Schema can either extend or restrict the base type. A "dummy" intermediate type has to be used to model full top-down inheritance of attributes with both extending and restricting derivations. For example, it is not possible to model a student as a person with a student number and *age* < 40 in only one step. You first have to model a dummy type "young person", which restricts the age of persons to less than 40. After that it is possible to model a student as a "young person" extended with a student number.

The bottom-up inheritance of instances to superclasses is also not automatically available in XML Schema. For example, an instance of a student is not automatically a valid instance of a person, even if the student type inherits from the person type.

Up to now we have discussed the mapping from ontologies to DTDs. [Welty & Ide, 1999] discuss a mapping from DTDs to an ontological representation. Their aim is to provide the reasoning service of description logic to query and manipulate XML documents. DTDs are therefore translated automatically into a representation of an ontology in description logic. This ontology simply consists of each element in the DTD. The taxonomy can be derived by the classifier of the description logic CLASSIC based on the use of entities and type attributes.

3.4.2   RDF And Ontologies

RDF and RDFS can be used directly to describe an ontology. *Objects*, *classes*, and *properties* can be described. Predefined properties can be used to model *instance of* and *subclass of* relationships as well as *domain restrictions* and *range restrictions* of attributes. A speciality of RDFS is that properties are defined globally and are not encapsulated as attributes in class definitions. Therefore, a frame or object-oriented ontology can only be expressed in RDFS by reifying the property names with class name suffixes (as we have already seen for XML). In regard to ontologies, RDF provides two important contributions:

- a standardized syntax for writing ontologies;
- a standard set of modeling primitives like *instance of* and *subclass of* relationships.

On the one hand, RDFS provides rather limited expressive power. A serious weakness of RDF is that it lacks a standard for describing logical axioms. RDFS allows the definition of classes and properties through their types (by providing their names). No intensional definitions or complex relationships via axioms can be defined. On the other hand, RDFS provides a rather strong reification mechanism. RDF expressions can be used as terms in meta-expressions. Here, RDFS provides reified second-order logic as used in CycL and KIF. Neither Frame Logic nor most description logics provide such an expressivity.[15] However, there are good reasons for this restriction in the latter approaches. This feature makes it very difficult to define a clean semantics in the framework of first-order logic and disables sound and complete inference services.[16] In the case of RDFS, such an inference service remains possible because of the otherwise restricted expressive power that

---

[15] Exceptions are described in [Calvanese et al., 1995] and [De Giacomo & Lenzerini, 1995], however, without an implemented reasoning service.

[16] The problems stem from the fact that, because terms in second-order logic may be arbitrary formulas, term unification in second-order logic (i.e., one simple sub step in deduction) requires full deduction in first-order logic which is undecidable in the general case.

does not provide any rule language. That is, RDFS provides syntactical features of second-order logic without actually requiring second-order semantics.

3.4.3   Comparing RDF and XML

RDF is an application of XML for the purpose of representing metadata. For example, the RDF statements:

```
date(http://www.xyz.de/Example/Smith/) = July 1999
subject(http://www.xyz.de/Example/Smith/) = Intelligent
   Agents
creator(http://www.xyz.de/Example/Smith/) = http://
   www.xyz.de/~smith/
name(http://www.xyz.de/~smith/) = John Smith
email(http://www.xyz.de/~smith/) = smith@organisation.de
```

can be represented in linear XML syntax (see Fig. 9). This may raise the question why there is a need for RDF at all, because all metadata represented in RDF can also be represented in XML. However, RDF provides a *standard* form for representing metadata in XML. Directly using XML to represent metadata would result in its being represented in various ways.

The difference becomes even more obvious when considering how to represent an ontology in RDF or XML. Earlier we discussed how an ontology can be used to generate a DTD describing the structure of XML documents.

```
<? xml version="1.0" ?>
<RDF
   xmlns="http://www.w3c.org/1999/02/22-rdf-syntax-ns#"
   xmlns:DC="http://www.purl.org/DC#/"
   xmlns:y="http://www.description.org/schema">
   <Description about="http://www.xyz.de/Example/Smith/">
       <DC:date rdf:resource="July 1999"/>
       <DC:subject rdf:resource="Intelligent Agents"/>
       <DC:creator rdf:resource="http://www.xyz.de/~smith/"/>
   </Description>
   <Description about="http://www.xyz.de/~smith/">
       <DC:name rdf:resource="John Smith"/>
       <DC:email rdf:resource="smith@organisation.de"/>
   </Description>
</RDF>
```

Fig. 9   XML representation of RDF statements

However, we did not discuss how the ontology itself could be represented in XML. To define a standardized manner in which ontologies can be represented in XML we have to address two questions:

- What are the epistemological primitives used to represent an ontology (i.e., things like classes, is-a relationships, element-of relationships, attributes, domain and range restrictions etc.)? Basically these are decisions about the *meta*-ontology used to represent ontologies.

- How can these concepts be represented in the linear syntax of XML?

There are a number of different possibilities, and this makes clear how RDFS comes into the story. RDFS provides a fixed set of modeling primitives for defining an ontology (classes, resources, properties, is-a and element-of relationships, etc.) and a standard way to encode them in XML. Using XML directly for the purpose of representing ontologies would require us to duplicate this standardization effort.

3.5   New Standards

Currently several proposals have been made to unify ontology and Web languages. We will conclude our discussion by briefly dealing with these new approaches.

3.5.1   XOL

The BioOntology Core Group[17] recommends the use of a *frame-based* language with an *XML syntax* for the exchange of ontologies for molecular biology. The proposed language is called XOL[18] (see [Karp et al., 1999], [McEntire et al., 1999]). The ontology definitions that XOL is designed to encode include both schema information (metadata), such as class definitions from object databases – as well as non-schema information (ground facts), such as object definitions from object databases.

The syntax of XOL is based on XML. The modeling primitives and semantics of XOL are based on OKBC-Lite, which is a simplified form of the knowledge model for *Open Knowledge Base Connectivity (OKBC)*[19] ([Chaudhri et al., 1997], [Chaudhri et al., 1998]). OKBC is an application

---

[17] http://smi-web.stanford.edu/projects/bio-Ontology
[18] http://www.Ontologos.org/Ontology/XOL.htm
[19] http://www.ai.sri.com/~okbc. OKBC has also been chosen by FIPA as its exchange standard for ontologies; see http://www.fipa.org, FIPA 98 Specification, Part 12 Ontology Service (see [FIPA 98, part 12]).

```
<class>
  <name>person</name>
</class>
<slot>
  <name>age</name>
  <domain>person</domain>
  <value-type>integer</value-type>
  <numeric-max>150</numeric-max>
</slot>
<individual>
  <name>fred</name>
  <type>person</type>
  <slot-values>
  <name>age</name>
  <value>35</value>
  </slot-values>
</individual>
```

Fig. 10   An example in XOL (taken from [Karp et al., 1999])

program interface for accessing frame knowledge representation systems. Its knowledge model supports features most commonly found in knowledge representation systems, object databases, and relational databases. OKBC-Lite extracts most of the essential features of OKBC, but omits some of its more complex aspects. XOL was inspired by Ontolingua. It differs from Ontolingua, however, as it has an XML-based syntax rather than a Lisp-based syntax.

The design of XOL deliberately uses a generic approach to define ontologies, meaning that the single set of XML tags defined for XOL (defined by a single XML DTD) can describe any and every ontology. This approach contrasts with the approaches taken by other XML schema languages, in which a generic set of tags is typically used to define the schema portion of the ontology and the schema itself is used to generate a second set of application-specific tags (and an application-specific DTD), which in turn are used to encode a separate XML file that contains the data portion of the ontology. Compare the XOL definitions in Figure 10. All of the XML elements of this specification (meaning all the words inside brackets), such as *class*, *individual*, and *name*, are generic, i.e., they pertain to all ontologies. All of the ontology-specific information is in the text portion of the XML file, i.e., between the pairs of elements. In contrast, approaches discussed earlier in this book might use this type of XML markup to define the individual Fred as shown in Figure 11.

What are the advantages of the generic approach taken by XOL relative to the non-generic approach? The primary advantage of the XOL approach is simplicity. Only one XML DTD need be defined to describe any and every ontology. Using the non-generic approach, every ontology must define a second, ontology-specific, DTD for describing the data elements of the ontology. Furthermore, rules would have to be defined that describe exactly how that second DTD is derived from the schema portion of the ontology, and most likely, programs would have to be written to generate such DTDs from schema specifications. The XML language provides no formal machinery to define those rules. The entire DTD defining *valid* XOL documents is given in Figure 12. XOL appears interesting because it provides ontological modeling primitives expressed in one of the most important information exchange standards, XML.

3.5.2   OIL

OIL[20] (see [Fensel et al., 2001], [Fensel et al., 2000(b)]) unifies three important paradigms provided by different communities (see Fig. 13): formal semantics and efficient reasoning support as provided by description logics; epistemologically rich modeling primitives as provided by the frame community; and a standard proposal for syntactical exchange notation as provided by the Web community.

Description Logics. Description Logics describe knowledge in terms of concepts and role restrictions that are used to automatically derive classification taxonomies. In spite of the discouraging theoretical complexity of their results, there are now efficient implementations for DL languages; see, for example, DLP[21] and the FaCT system.[22] OIL inherits from description logic its *formal semantics* and the *efficient reasoning support* developed for these languages. In OIL, *subsumption* is decidable and with FaCT we can provide an efficient reasoner for this.

Frame–based systems. The central modeling primitives of predicate logic are predicates. Frame-based and object-oriented approaches take a different point of view. Their central modeling primitives are classes (i.e., frames) with certain properties called attributes. These attributes do not have a global

```
<person>
   <name>fred</name>
   <age>35</age>
</person>
```

Fig. 11   Non-reusable ontology specification

---

[20] http://www.ontoknowledge.org/oil
[21] http://www.bell-labs.com/user/pfps
[22] http://www.cs.man.ac.uk/~horrocks/FaCT. Actually OIL uses FaCT as its inference engine.

```
<!ELEMENT
   (module | ontology | kb | database | dataset)
   ( name, (kb-type | db-type)?, package?, version?,
   documentation?, class*, slot*, individual*)>
<!ELEMENT name (#PCDATA)>
<!ELEMENT kb-type (#PCDATA)>
<!ELEMENT documentation (#PCDATA)>
<!ELEMENT class
   ( name, documentation?,
   (subclass-of | instance-of | slot-values)* )>
<!ELEMENT slot
   ( name, documentation?,
   (domain | slot-value-type | slot-inverse | slot-cardinality |
slot-maximum-cardinality |
   slot-minimum-cardinality | slot-numeric-minimum | slot-
   numeric-maximum | slot-collection-type | slot-values)* )>
<!ATTLIST slot
   type ( template | own ) "own">
<!ELEMENT individual
   ( name, documentation?, (type | slot-values)* )>
<!ELEMENT slot-values
   ( name, value*,
   (facet-values | value-type | inverse
   | cardinality | maximum-cardinality | minimum-cardinality
   | numeric-minimum | numeric-maximum | some-values
   | collection-type | documentation-in-frame)* )>
<!ELEMENT facet-values
   ( name, value* )
<!ELEMENT subclass-of (#PCDATA)>
<!ELEMENT instance-of (#PCDATA)>
<!ELEMENT domain (#PCDATA)>
<!ELEMENT slot-value-type (#PCDATA)>
<!ELEMENT slot-inverse (#PCDATA)>
<!ELEMENT slot-cardinality (#PCDATA)>
<!ELEMENT slot-maximum-cardinality (#PCDATA)>
<!ELEMENT slot-minimum-cardinality (#PCDATA)>
<!ELEMENT slot-numeric-minimum (#PCDATA)>
<!ELEMENT slot-numeric-maximum (#PCDATA)>
<!ELEMENT slot-collection-type (#PCDATA)>
<!ELEMENT value-type (#PCDATA)>
<!ELEMENT inverse (#PCDATA)>
<!ELEMENT cardinality (#PCDATA)>
<!ELEMENT maximum-cardinality (#PCDATA)>
<!ELEMENT minimum-cardinality (#PCDATA)>
<!ELEMENT numeric-minimum (#PCDATA)>
<!ELEMENT numeric-maximum (#PCDATA)>
<!ELEMENT some-values (#PCDATA)>
```

Fig. 12   The XOL DTD (see http://www.ontologos.org/Ontology/XOL.htm)

scope but are only applicable to the classes they are defined for (they are typed), and the "same" attribute (i.e., the same attribute name) may be associated with different range and value restrictions when defined for different classes. A frame provides a certain context for modeling one aspect of a domain. Many other additional refinements of these modeling constructs have been developed and have led to the great success of this modeling paradigm. Many frame-based systems and languages have been developed and, renamed as object-orientation, they have conquered the software engineering community. Therefore, OIL incorporates the *essential modeling primitives* of frame-based systems into its language. OIL is based on the notion of a concept and the definition of its superclasses and attributes. Relations can also be defined not only as an attribute of a class but also as an independent entity having a certain domain and range. Like classes, relations can be arranged in a hierarchy.

Web standards: XML and RDF. Modeling primitives and their semantics are one aspect of an ontology language. Next, we have to decide about its syntax. Given the current dominance and importance of the WWW, a syntax of an ontology exchange language must be formulated using existing Web standards for information representation. OIL is closely related to XOL and can be seen as an extension of it. For example, XOL only allows necessary but not sufficient class definitions (i.e., a new class is always a subclass of, and not exactly equal to, its specification) and only class names, but not class expressions (except for the limited form of expression provided by slots and their facets), can be used in defining classes. The XML syntax of OIL was mainly defined as an extension of XOL. Another candidate for a Web-based syntax for OIL is RDF together with RDFS. In regard to ontologies, RDFS

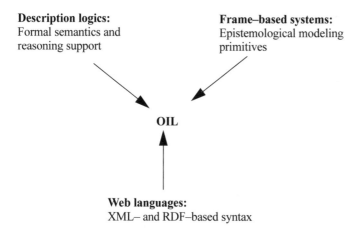

Fig. 13   The three roots of OIL

provides two important contributions: a standardized syntax for writing ontologies, and a standard set of modeling primitives like instance-of and subclass-of relationships. Therefore, OIL offers two syntactical variants: one based on XML schema and one based on RDF schema.

3.5.3   DAML+OIL

DAML+OIL[23] builds on work from the OIL initiatives (see [McGuinness et al., 2002]). It provides modeling primitives commonly found in frame-based languages (such as an asserted subsumption hierarchy and the description or definition of classes through slot fillers) and has a clean and well-defined semantics. DAML+OIL is effectively an alternative presentation syntax for a description logic (SHIQ with the addition of concrete data types) with an underlying RDFS-based delivery mechanism. The presence of the well-defined semantics in terms of SHIQ allow the use of description logic reasoners such as FaCT[24] or RACER,[25] in particular to support the tasks of classification and inconsistency detection. The development of DAML+OIL was the responsibility of the Joint US/EU ad hoc Agent Markup Language Committee.[26] Many members of that committee are now part of the WebOnt Committee which we will explain in the next section.

3.5.4   The Web Ontology Language OWL

The **W3C Web Ontology Working Group**,[27] part of the W3C's Semantic Web Activity,[28] has focused on the development of a language to extend the semantic reach of current XML and RDF metadata efforts. The working group builds the Ontological layer necessary for developing applications that depend on an understanding of logical content, not just human-readable presentation, and the formal underpinnings thereof. Specifically, the Web Ontology Working Group is chartered to design a Web Ontology language, which builds on current Web languages that allow the specification of classes and subclasses, properties and subproperties (such as RDFS), but which extends these constructs to allow more complex relationships between entities including: the means to limit the properties of classes with respect to number and type; the means to infer that items with various properties are

---

[23] http://www.daml.org/2001/03/daml+oil–index.html
[24] http://www.cs.man.ac.uk/fact
[25] http://kogs–www.informatik.uni–hamburg.de/~race
[26] http://www.daml.org/committee
[27] http://www.w3.org/2001/sw/WebOnt
[28] http://www.w3.org/2001/sw

members of a particular class; a well-defined model of property inheritance; and similar semantic extensions to the base languages.

The *Web Ontology Language (OWL) Reference Draft* [Dean et al., 2002] provides the OWL Web Ontology Language specification. OWL is derived from the DAML+OIL language and builds upon RDFS. Because this language is still under development, we refer the interested reader to the websites of the W3C: http://www.w3.org/2001/sw/WebOnt.

When comparing OIL and OWL the following main aspects are apparent:

- OIL had two syntactical definitions: one in plain XML (based on XML schema) and one in RDFS. The reason was that OIL did not want to completely subscribe to the RDFS world, leaving the much larger XML world behind. OWL subscribes to RDFS only.

- Both OIL and OWL are layered languages. OWL-Lite [McGuinness & van Harmelen, 2002] defines a subset of OWL. Unfortunately this subset is not defined in a well-thought manner. One would expect that the simple sublanguage does not require a description logic type of reasoner. However, the fact that cardinality constraints can be used to derive equalities of terms requires DL-based reasoning to decide whether two terms are equal (instead of simple term unification in standard logical reasoning). On the one hand, this makes even the simple sublanguage complex to deal with. On the other hand, it does not add anything to its usage. It is bizarre to model equality of terms via cardinality constraints and one needs much richer means to express equality of terms anyway than cardinality constraints or factual equality statements. From our point of view it would have been much wiser to assume non-equality of terms (i.e., the unique-name assumption of the database area) and provide a much more powerful oracle beyond the ontology language that normalizes different terms that denote the same thing.

- OIL and OWL are based on description logic, however, it has never been proven that it is the appropriate logical paradigm for the Semantic Web. OIL combined a description logic with a frame-based orientation. OWL is more an RDF(S) syntax for a description logic.

XOL, OIL, DAML+OIL, and OWL represent different points in the coordination system of Web ontology languages. Table 1 summarizes our comparison. In a sense, only OWL has any chance of survival. However, future usage of OWL may require adaptations that will be easier if some of the different design decisions are kept in mind.

Table 1. Summarizing language features

	XOL	OIL	DAML+OIL	OWL
XML–based	+	+		
RDF(S)–based		+	+	+
Frame–based	+	+		
DL–based		+	+	+
Layered		+		"+"
Alive	No	No	No	Yes

4 Tools

This chapter describes tools that help us to work with ontologies and to apply them to improve information access. We start with a general survey on various aspects of ontology tooling and give examples. Then we describe a tool that was among the first to merge the ontology paradigm with the Web, helping to create the research field that is now called the Semantic Web. Its description gives us an example that illustrates the different requirements to make ontology technology work. Then we discuss some professional tools now available on the market.

4.1 A Survey

Effective and efficient work with ontologies must be supported by advanced tools enabling the full power of this technology. In particular, we need the following elements:

- Ontology languages to express and represent ontologies.
- Ontology editors and semi-automatic ontology construction to build new ontologies.
- Reuse and merging of ontologies, i.e., ontology environments that help to create new ontologies by reusing existing ones.
- Reasoning with ontologies: Instance and schema inferences to enable advanced query answering services, support ontology creation and help to map between different ontologies.
- Ontology-based annotation tools to enable unstructured and semistructured information sources to be linked with ontologies.
- Ontology-based tools for information access and navigation to enable intelligent information access for human users.

We will now discuss these elements in some details.

4.1.1   Ontology Languages

Ontology languages must fulfill three important requirements:

- They must be highly intuitive to the human user. Given the current success of the frame-based and object-oriented modeling paradigm, they should have a frame-like look and feel.

- They must have a well-defined formal semantics with established reasoning properties in terms of completeness, correctness, and efficiency.

- They must have a proper link with existing Web languages like XML and RDF, ensuring interoperability.

A more detailed discussion of these aspects was provided in the chapter 3.

4.1.2   Ontology Editors and Semi–automatic Ontology Construction

Ontology editors help human knowledge engineers to build ontologies. Ontology editors support the definition of concept hierarchies, the definition attributes for concepts, and the definition of axioms and constraints. They must provide graphical interfaces and must conform to existing standards in Web-based software development. They enable inspection, browsing, codification and modification of ontologies and thus support their development and maintenance. Examples are:

- *Protégé*[1] (see [Grosso et al., 1999]) and Protégé-2000 (see [Puerta et al., 1992], [Erikson et al., 1999]) are versions of a series of tools developed by the Knowledge Modeling Group at Stanford Medical Informatics to assist developers in the construction of large electronic knowledge bases (see Figure 14). Protégé allows developers to create, browse and edit domain ontologies in a frame-based representation, which is compliant with the OKBC knowledge model [Chaudhri et al., 1998]. Starting with an ontology, Protégé automatically constructs a graphical knowledge-acquisition tool that allows application specialists to enter the detailed content knowledge required to define specific applications. Protégé allows developers to customize this knowledge-acquisition tool directly by arranging and configuring the graphical entities in forms that are attached to each class in the ontology for the acquisition of instances. This allows application specialists to enter domain information by filling

---

[1] http://www.smi.stanford.edu/projects/protege

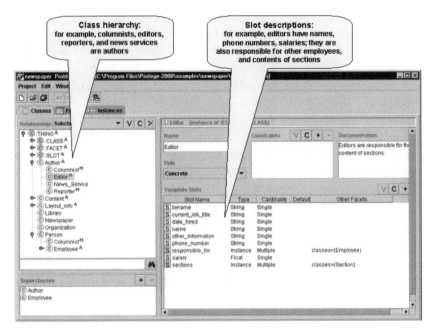

Fig. 14   Protégé

in the blanks of intuitive forms and by drawing diagrams composed of selectable icons and connectors. Protégé-2000 allows knowledge bases to be stored in several formats, among others RDF.

- *OntoEdit*[2] [Sure et al., 2002] is an ontology engineering environment developed at the Knowledge Management Group of the University of Karlsruhe. Currently OntoEdit supports representation languages such as F-logic, OIL, and RDFS. It is marketed by Ontoprise[3].

- *WebOnto*[4] is a Java applet coupled with a customized Web server which allows users to browse and edit ontologies over the Web. The resulting Planet-Onto architecture provides an integrated set of tools to support news publishing, ontology-driven document formalization, story identification and personalized news feeds and alerts. It was developed at the Knowledge Media Institute of the Open University in Milton Keynes.

---

[2] http://ontoserver.aifb.uni–karlsruhe.de/ontoedit
[3] http://www.ontoprise.de
[4] http://kmi.open.ac.uk/projects/webonto

- *OilEd*[5] is a simple editor that allows the user to create and edit OIL ontologies. The main intention behind OilEd is to provide a simple, freeware editor that demonstrates the use of, and stimulates interest in, DAML+OIL. OilEd is not intended as a full ontology development environment – it will not actively support the development of large-scale ontologies, the migration and integration of ontologies, versioning, argumentation and many other activities that are involved in ontology construction. It should, however, provide enough to allow the basic construction of OIL ontologies and demonstrate the power of the connection to the FaCT reasoner. Both tools were developed at the University of Manchester, UK.

- *ODE* (Ontology Design Environment)[6] is a software tool for specifying ontologies at a high conceptual level. ODE allows developers to specify their ontology by filling in tables and drawing graphs. Its multilingual generator module automatically translates the specification of the ontology into target languages. It was developed at the University of Madrid.

- Many authors recommend UML as a representation language (see, for example, [Cranefield & Purvis, 1999]) for ontologies. The advantage of using UML development environments is that standard software development tools can be used to build ontologies. A disadvantage is that such tools may provide less support than customized special-purpose ontology editors.

Manually building ontologies is a time-consuming task. It is very difficult and cumbersome to manually derive ontologies from data. This appears to be true even regardless of the type of data one might consider. Natural language texts exhibit morphological, syntactic, semantic, pragmatic and conceptual constraints that interact in order to convey a particular meaning to the reader. Thus, the text transports information to the reader and the reader embeds this information into his background knowledge. Tools that learn ontologies from natural language exploit the interacting constraints on the various language levels (from morphology to pragmatics and background knowledge) in order to discover new concepts and stipulate relationships between concepts. Therefore, in addition to editor support, semi-automated tools in ontology development help to improve the overall productivity. These tools combine machine learning, information extraction and linguistic techniques. The main tasks are:

---

[5] http://oiled.man.ac.uk
[6] http://delicias.dia.fi.upm.es/miembros/ASUN/asun_CV_Esp.html

- extraction of relevant concepts;

- building is-a hierarchies;

- extraction relationships between concepts.

A review of the state of the art on ontology learning was presented at an ECAI workshop in Berlin during August 2000.[7] Example systems are:

- *Asium*, which stands for "Acquisition of SemantIc knowledge Using Machine learning method". The main aim of Asium is to help the expert in the acquisition of semantic knowledge from texts and to generalize the knowledge of the corpus. Asium provides the expert with a powerful and user-friendly interface which will first help him or her to explore the texts and then to learn knowledge which is not in the texts.

- The *Text-To-Onto system*, which provides an integrated environment for the task of learning ontologies learning from text (see Figure 15). The Text Management module enables a relevant corpus to be selected. These domain texts may be both natural language texts and HTML formatted texts. For a meaningful analysis text has to be preprocessed. The Text Management module serves as an interface to the Information Extraction Server. If a domain lexicon already exists, the information extraction server performs domain specific parsing. The results of the parsing process are stored in XML or feature-value structures. The Management Module offers all existing learning components to the user. Typically these components are parametrizable. Existing knowledge structures (e.g., a taxonomy of concepts) are incorporated as background knowledge. The learning component discovers on the basis of the domain texts new knowledge structures, which are collected in the ontology modeling module to expand the existing ontology. Text-To-Onto was developed by the Knowledge Management Group of University of Karlsruhe.

4.1.3   Reusing and Merging Ontologies: Ontology Environments

Assuming that the world is full of well-designed modular ontologies, constructing a new ontology is a matter of assembling existing ones. Instead of building ontologies from scratch one wants to reuse existing ontologies. Tools that best support this approach allow for the adaptation and merging of existing ontologies to fit them for new tasks and domains. The knowledge engineer needs support in merging multiple ontologies and diagnosing

---

[7] http://ol2000.aifb.uni-karlsruhe.de

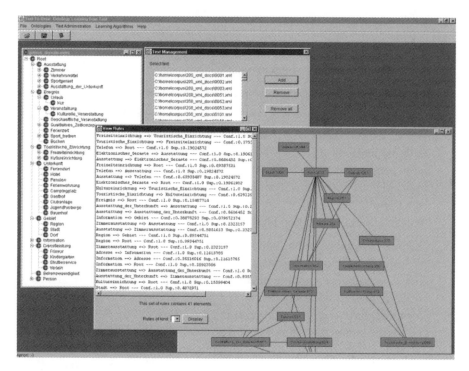

Fig. 15   Ontotext

individual or multiple ontologies. He requires support in such tasks as using ontologies in differing formats, reorganizing taxonomies, resolving name conflicts, browsing ontologies, editing terms, etc. Possible solution providers for ontology environments are the following:

- [Farquhar et al., 1997] describes the *Ontolingua* server, which provides different kinds of operations for combining ontologies: inclusion; restriction; and polymorphic refinement. For example, inclusion of one ontology in another has the effect that the resulting ontology consists of the union of the two ontologies (their classes, relations, axioms).

- The *SENSUS* system [Swartout et al., 1996] provides a means for constructing a domain-specific ontology from given common-sense ontologies. The basic idea is to use so-called seed elements which represent the most important domain concepts for identifying the relevant parts of a top-level ontology. The selected parts are then used as starting points for extending the ontology with further domain-specific concepts.

- The *SKC* project (Scalable Knowledge Composition) [Jannink et al., 1998] aims to develop an algebra for systematically composing ontologies from already existing ones. It will offer union, intersection, and difference as basic operations for such an algebra.

- *Chimaera* provides support for two important tasks: (1) merging multiple ontologies and (2) diagnosing (and evolving) ontologies [McGuinness et al., 2000]. We will describe this system in more detail below.

- *PROMT* (formally known as SMART) is an interactive ontology-merging tool [Noy & Musen, 2000]. It guides the user through the merging process, making suggestions, determining conflicts, and proposing conflict-resolution strategies. PROMPT starts with the linguistic similarity matches of frame names for the initial comparison, but concentrates on finding clues based on the structure of the ontology and the user's actions. After the user selects an operation to perform, PROMPT determines the conflicts in the merged ontology that the operation has caused and proposes possible solutions to the conflicts. It then considers the structure of the ontology around the arguments to the latest operations–relations among the arguments and other concepts in the ontology–and proposes other operations that the user should perform. In the PROMPT project, a set of knowledge-base operations for ontology merging or alignment is identified. For each operation in this set the following is defined: (1) the changes that PROMPT performs automatically; (2) the new suggestions that PROMPT presents to the user; and (3) the conflicts that the operation may introduce and that the user needs to resolve. When the user invokes an operation, PROMPT creates members of these three sets based on the arguments to the specific invocation of the operation.

- *OntoMorph* [Chalupsky, 2000] is a transformation system for symbolic knowledge. It facilitates ontology merging and the rapid generation of knowledge-base translators. It combines two mechanisms to describe knowledge-base transformations: (1) syntactic rewriting via pattern-directed rewrite rules that allow the concise specification of sentence-level transformations based on pattern matching; and (2) semantic rewriting which modulates syntactic rewriting via (partial) semantic models and logical inference via an integrated knowledge representation system. The integration of these mechanisms allows transformations to be based on any mixture of syntactic and semantic criteria. The OntoMorph architecture facilitates incremental development and scripted replay of transformations, which is particularly important during merging operations. OntoMorph focusses on the transformations to individual ontologies that are needed to bring two or more ontologies into mutual agreement. This is a small but important step in the process of merging ontologies. OntoMorph is able to solve several problems at the language level of ontology mismatches. Of course, a difference in expressivity between two languages is not solvable and may imply loss of knowledge. Solutions for ontology-level problems can also be formulated in OntoMorph. Because OntoMorph requires a clear and executable specification of the transformation, the process can be repeated with modified versions of the original ontologies. To summarize with OntoMorph it is possible to specify the transformations of an ontology, both at a syntactical level and semantic level, which can be carried out automatically.

- *OntoView* [Klein et al., 2002] is a Web-based system that provides support for the versioning of online ontologies, which might help to solve some of the problems of evolving ontologies on the Web. Its main function is to help the user to manage changes in ontologies and to keep different ontology versions as much interoperable as possible. It does this by comparing versions of ontologies and highlighting the differences. It then allows the user to specify the conceptual relation between the different versions of concepts. It also provides a transparent interface to arbitrary versions of ontologies. To achieve this, the system maintains an internal specification of the relation between the different variants of ontologies: it keeps track of the metadata, the conceptual relations between constructs in the ontologies and the transformations between them. OntoView has been inspired by the Concurrent Versioning System (CVS), used in software development to allow collaborative development of source code.

Further approaches are described in [Amann & Fundulaki, 1999] and [Weinstein & Birmingham, 1999].

Figure 16 illustrates Chimeara from the University of Stanford.[8] Chimaera is primarily intended as a tool for merging knowledge-base fragments. The process of knowledge-base merging typically involves such activities as resolving name conflicts and aligning the taxonomy. To this end, this tool has special support for finding name conflicts and for walking the user through the merged taxonomy, pointing out likely places for your attention.

- **Taxonomic relationships**. The primary function of Chimaera is to set up taxonomic relationships. There are two types of subclass-of relationship:

---

[8] A summary of the Chimaera documentation from which we quote is available at http:// www-ksl-svc.stanford.edu:5915/doc/chimaera/chimaera-docs.html.

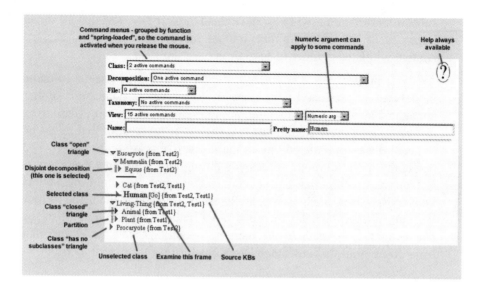

Fig. 16   Chimaera

direct and indirect. The indirect subclass is derived through several direct subclass-of relations using transitivity of the relation. The merger allows you to arrange only direct taxonomic relationships and does not support indirect subclass-of relation.

- **Decompositions**. Chimaera has special features for capturing and displaying three types of class decomposition. The first type is disjoint decomposition, where the subclasses in question are disjoint from one another. In exhaustive decomposition the subclasses exhaustively cover the subclasses of the class in question. Any subclass of the class in question must be a subclass of one of these classes. Finally, in partition the subclasses are all mutually disjoint, and exhaustively cover the subclasses of the class in question. A partition is therefore an exhaustive, disjoint decomposition.

- **Slots**. Chimaera has facilities for manipulating not only the taxonomic relationships between classes, but also the slots (attributes) of those classes. Chimaera recognizes two distinct types of slots: own slots and template slots. Own slots are slots that specify properties of the object itself, as opposed to properties of instances of a class. Own slots on classes are just like own slots on individuals; they say things about the class itself. Template slots are slots defined on classes that are manifested on instances of those classes. For example, we might define the template slot number-of-legs on the class Animal. This means that all subclasses of Animal will also have this template slot, and that all direct instances of the class Animal and all instances of all subclasses of Animal will have number-of-legs as an own slot.

- **Analysis modes**. There are three different modes in Chimaera. In name mode you are presented with pairs of classes whose names are similar enough in some way that they might represent either the same class from different input knowledge bases that should be merged, or that might be in need of a taxonomic editing to make one a subclass of the other. The taxonomy traversal mode guides you through the taxonomy causing you to look at any class that has subclasses that came from multiple source knowledge bases. Such classes are likely places for the inclusion of new decompositions. The slot traversal mode guides you through all of the classes that, as a result of the merging operations, now have slots that came from multiple knowledge bases. Such slots might need merging.

4.1.4   Reasoning with Ontologies: Instance and Schema Inferences

Inference engines for ontologies can be used to reason about instances of an ontology or over ontology schemes.

Reasoning over instances of an ontology, for example, deriving a certain value for an attribute applied to an object. Such inference service can be used to answer queries about explicit and implicit knowledge specified by an ontology. The powerful support in formulating rules, constraints and answering queries about schema information is far beyond existing database technology. These inference services are the equivalent of SQL query engines for databases, however provide stronger support (for example, recursive rules). Example systems are: CLIPS[9] (used as one output format of Protégé), SWI Prolog,[10] Ontobroker,[11] and Flora[12]. Alternatively, simpler RDF query engines[13] based on database technology can be used. They provide less problems in scalability, but restrict the expressive power for rules, queries, and the way they access the concept definitions of an ontology (e.g., they may ignore inheritance).

Reasoning over concepts of an ontology, for example, automatically deriving the right position of a new concept in a given concept hierarchy. FaCT (Fast Classification of Terminologies)[14] can be used to automatically

---

[9] CLIPS: A Tool for Building Expert Systems. http://www.ghgcorp.com/clips/CLIPS.html
[10] http://www.swi.psy.uva.nl/projects/SWI–Prolog
[11] http://www.ontoprise.de
[12] http://www.cs.sunysb.edu/~sbprolog/flora
[13] A survey of RDF query engines can be found at [Broekstra et al., 2000].

derive concept hierarchies. It is a description logic classifier that makes use of the well-defined semantics of OIL.

Both types of reasoners help to build ontologies and to use them for advanced information access and navigation, as we will discuss below.

4.1.5   Ontology – based Annotation Tools

Ontologies can be used to describe large document collections. Tools need to help the knowledge engineer to establish large amounts of links between ontologies and documents via:

- linking an ontology with a database schema or deriving a database schema from an ontology in the case of structured data;

- deriving an XML DTD, an XML schema, and an RDF schema from an ontology in the case of semistructured data;

- manually or semi-automatically adding Ontological annotation to unstructured data.

More details can be found in [Erdmann & Studer, 2001] and [Klein et al., 2000].

4.1.6   Using Ontologies for Information Access and Navigation

Work with the Web is currently done at a very low level: clicking on links and using keyword search for links is the main (if not the only) navigation technique. It is like programming with assembler and go-to instructions. Such a low-level interface may significantly hamper the expected future growth of the Web.

- Keyword-based search retrieves irrelevant information that uses a certain word in a different sense or it may miss information where different words are used to describe the desired content. Navigation is only supported by predefined links and does not support clustering and linking of pages based on semantic similarity.

- The query responses require human browsing and reading to extract the relevant information from these information sources. This burdens Web users with an additional loss of time and seriously limits information retrieval by automatic agents that miss all common-sense knowledge required to extract such information from textual representations.

---

[14] http://www.cs.man.ac.uk/~horrocks/FaCT

- Keyword-based document retrieval fails to integrate information spread over different sources.

- Finally, current retrieval services can only retrieve information that is located explicitly on the Web. No further inference service is provided for deriving implicit information.

Ontologies help to overcome such bottlenecks in information access. They support information retrieval based on the actual content of a page. They help to navigate the information space based on semantic concepts. They enable advanced query answering and information extraction services, integrating heterogeneous and distributed information sources enriched by inferred background knowledge. Ontology technology provides two major improvements:

- Semantic information visualization does not group information by location but by content. Examples are the hyperbolic browsing interface of Ontoprise[15] and the page content visualization tool of Aidministrator[16] (see Figure 17).

- Query answering service for semistructured information sources.

In the following, we will discuss some of these aspects in more detail.

4.2   Ontobroker and On2broker: Early Research Prototypes

Ontobroker (see [Fensel et al., 1998(a)], [Decker et al., 1999]) applies artificial intelligence techniques to improve access to heterogeneous, scattered and semistructured information sources as they are presented on the World Wide Web or organization-wide intranets. It relies on the use of ontologies to annotate Web pages, formulate queries, and derive answers. Basically you define an ontology and use it to annotate/structure/wrap your Web documents, and somebody else can make use of Ontobroker's advanced query and inference services to consult your knowledge. To achieve this goal, Ontobroker provides three interleaved languages and two tools. It provides a broker architecture with three core elements: a query interface for formulating queries; an inference engine used to derive answers; and a webcrawler to collect the required knowledge from the Web. It provides a *representation* language for formulating ontologies. A subset of this is used to formulate queries, i.e. to define the *query language*. An *annotation* language is offered to enable knowledge providers to enrich Web documents

---

[15] http://www.ontoprise.de
[16] http://www.aidministrator.nl

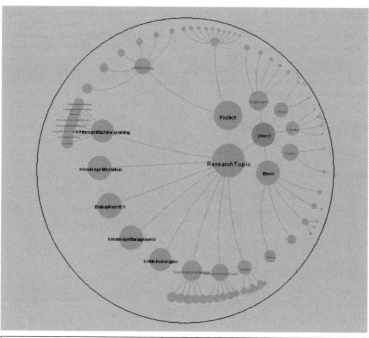

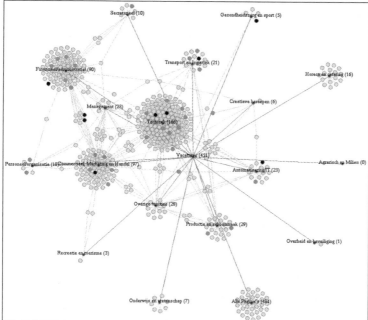

Fig. 17   Ontology-enabled information navigation

with Ontological information. The strength of Ontobroker is the close coupling of informal, semi-formal, and formal information and knowledge. This supports their maintenance and provides a service that can be used more generally for integrating knowledge-based reasoning with semi-formal documents.

4.2.1   The Languages

4.2.1.1 The Annotation Language

Ontobroker provides an *annotation* language called HTML^A to enable the annotation of HTML documents with machine-processable semantics. For example, the following HTML page states that the text string "Richard Benjamins" is the name of a researcher where the URL of his homepage is used as his object id.

```
<html><body>
   <a onto="page:Researcher"><h2>Welcome to my homepage</h2>
   My name is <a onto="[name=body]">Richard Benjamins</a>.
</body></html>
```

Two important design decision of HTML^A were (1) to smoothly integrate semantic annotations into HTML and (2) to prevent the duplication of information. The reason for the first decision was to lower the threshold for using the annotation language. People who are able to write HTML can use it straightforwardly as a simple extension. The pages remain readable by standard browsers like Netscape Navigator or Microsoft Explorer, and information providers can still rely on standard Web techniques. The rationale underlying the second decision is more fundamental in nature. We did not wish to add additional data, *instead we wished to make explicit the semantics of already available data*. The same piece of data (i.e., "Richard Benjamins") that is rendered by a browser is given a semantics saying that this ASCII string provides the name of a researcher. This is a significant difference between our approach and those of SHOE[17] [Luke et al. 1997], RDF [Lassila & Swick, 1999] and annotations used in information retrieval.

In Ontobroker, a frame-based approach has been chosen for the annotation language corresponding to the kind of language used for representing the ontology. Three primitives are provided to annotate Web documents:

- An *object* can be defined as an instance of a certain class.
- The *value* of an object's attribute can be set.
- A *relationship* between two or more objects may be established.

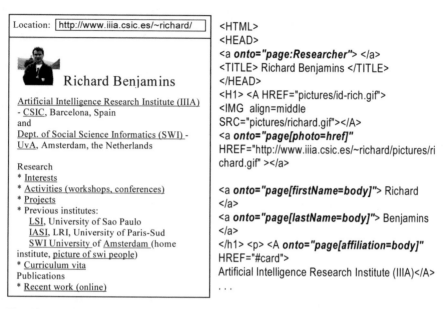

Fig. 18   An example of an annotated Web page

All three primitives are expressed by using an extended version of a frequent HTML tag, i.e. the anchor tag `<a ...> ... </a>`. The anchor tag is usually used to define named locations on a Web page and links to other locations. Thus, it contains the attributes *name* and *href* to fulfill these purposes. For ontologically annotating a Web page Ontobroker provides another attribute to the syntax of the anchor tag, namely the *onto* attribute. Typically, a provider of information first defines an object as an element of a certain class. To express this in its HTML extension he would use the following line on a home page:

```
<a onto='"http://www.iiia.csic.es/~richard":Researcher'>
</a>
```

URLs are used as object ids. Each class could possibly be associated with

---

[17] SHOE (see [Luke et al., 1996], [Luke et al. 1997]) introduced the idea of using ontologies for annotating Web sources. There are two main differences from Ontobroker. First, the annotation language is not used to annotate existing information on Web pages, but to add additional information and annotate them. That is, in SHOE information must be repeated and this redundancy may cause significant maintenance problems. For example, an affiliation must be provided once as a text string rendered by the browser and again as annotated metainformation. In this respect, SHOE is close to metatags in HTML. Ontobroker uses the annotations to directly add semantics to textual information that is also rendered by a browser. A second difference is the use of inference techniques and axioms to infer additional knowledge. SHOE relies only on database techniques. Therefore, no further inference service is provided. Ontobroker uses an inference engine to answer queries. Therefore, it can make use of rules that provide additional information.

a set of attributes. Each instance of a class can define values for these attributes. For example, the ontology contains an attribute email for each object of class Researcher. If Richard Benjamins wished to provide his email address, he would use this line on his home page:

```
<a onto='"http://www.iiia.csic.es/~richard"
[email=?mailto:richard@iiia.csic.es?]'></a>
```

The object denoted by "http://www.iiia.csic.es/~richard" has the value "mailto:richard@iiia.csic.es" for the attribute email. An example of an annotated Web page is given in Fig. 18.

In terms of a knowledge-based system, the annotation language provides the means to express factual knowledge (ground literals). Further knowledge is provided by the ontology. The ontology defines the terminology (i.e., signature) and may introduce further rules (i.e., axioms) that allow the derivation of additional facts that are not stated as extensions.

4.2.1.2 The Representation Languages

A *representation* language is used to formulate an ontology. This language is based on Frame logic [Kifer et al., 1995]. F-logic is a language for specifying object-oriented databases, frame systems, and logical programs. Its main achievement is to integrate conceptual modeling constructs (classes, attributes, domain and range restrictions, inheritance, axioms) into a coherent logical framework. Basically it provides classes, attributes with domain and range definitions, is-a hierarchies with set inclusion of subclasses and multiple attribute inheritance, and logical axioms that can be used to further characterize relationships between elements of an ontology and its instances. The representation language introduces the terminology that is used by the annotation language to define the factual knowledge provided by HTML pages on the Web. An example is provided in Figure 19. It defines the class *Object* and its subclasses *Person* and *Publication*. Some attributes and some rules expressing relationships between them are defined, for example, if a publication has a person as an author then respectively the author should have this publication as one of his publications. Semantically, the language for defining rules is the fragment of first-order logic that can be transformed via Lloyd-Topor transformations [Lloyd & Topor, 1984] into Horn logic. Syntactically it is different as it incorporates object-oriented modeling primitives. Ontobroker uses a subset of F-logic for defining the ontologies:

- Class definition:

    ```
    c[]
    ```
    defines a class with name c.

Class Hierarchy	Attribute Definitions	Rules

Object[].
 	
 Person :: Object.
 	
 Employee :: Person.
 	
 AcademicStaff :: Employee.
 	
 Researcher :: AcademicStaff.
 	
 Publication :: Object.
	Person[
	 firstName =>> STRING;
	 lastName =>> STRING;
	 eMail =>> STRING;
	 ...
	 publication =>> Publication].
	
	 Employee[
	 affiliation =>> Organization;
	 ...].
	
	 Researcher[
	 researchInterest =>> ResearchTopic;
	 ...].
		FORALL P_1, P_2
		 P_1[cooperatesWith ->> P_2]
		 <-
		 P_2[cooperatesWith->> P_1].
		
		 FORALL P, Pub
		 Pub:Publication
		 [author ->> P]
		 <->
		 P:Person
		 [publication ->> Pub].

Key to Figure 19:

c_1 :: c_2 means that c_1 is a subclass of c_2.

$c[a ==> r]$ means that an attribute a is of domain c and range r.

$o : c[a->> v]$ means that o is an element of c and has the value v for a.

<- means logical implication and <-> logical equivalence.

Fig. 19   An excerpt from an ontology (taken from [Benjamins et al., 1999])

- Attribute definition:

    $c[a=>> \{c_1, \ldots, c_n\}]$

    implies that the attribute a can be applied to the elements of c (it is also possible to define attributes applied to classes) and an attribute value must be member of all classes $c_1, \ldots, c_n$.

- Is-a relationship:

    c_1 :: c_2

    defines c_1 as a subclass of c_2 which implies that:

    - all elements of c_1 are also elements of c_2,

    - all attributes and their value restrictions defined for c_2 are also defined for c_1, and

- multiple attribute inheritance exists, i.e.
  ```
  c :: c₁[a =>> {c₃}] and c :: c₂[a =>> {c₄}] imply
  c[a =>> {c₃,c₄}]
  ```

- Is-element-of relationship:
  ```
  e : c
  ```
  defines e as an element of the class c.

- Rules like
  - ```
    FORALL x,y x[a ->> y] <- y[a ->> x].
    ```
  - ```
    FORALL x,y x:c₁[a₁ ->> y] <-> y:c₂[a₂ ->> x].
    ```

4.2.1.3 The Query Languages

The *query* language is defined as a subset of the representation language. The elementary expression is:

```
x ∈ c ∧ attribute(x) = v
```

Written in Frame logic as:

```
x[attribute -> v] : c
```

In the head of F-Logic rules, variables are all quantified. In the body, variables may be either all or existentially quantified. All quantified variables must additionally be bound by a positive atom in the body. Lloyd-Topor transformation handles these quantifications as follows. Existential quantifiers in the body may be dropped, because every variable in the body of a rule is implicitly existentially quantified. An all-quantification, *forall y p(y)*, in the body is transformed to

```
¬ exists y ¬ p(y).
```

Then Lloyd-Topor transformation produces a set of rules out of this. Queries are handled as rules without a head. Thus the above mentioned conditions for quantifications hold here too.

Complex expressions can be built by combing these elementary expressions with the usual logical connectives ($\land$, $\lor$, $\neg$). The following query asks for all abstracts of the publications of the researcher "Richard Benjamins".

```
x[name -> "Richard Benjamins"; publication ->> {y[abstract
-> z]}] : Researcher
```

The variable substitutions for z are the desired abstracts.

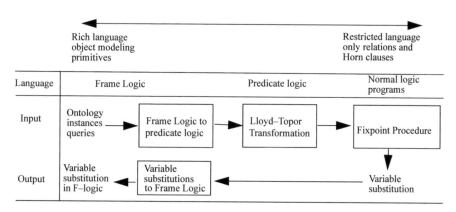

Fig. 20   Stages and languages used in the Inference Engine.

4.2.2   The Tools

Ontobroker relies on two tools that give it "life": a *webcrawler* and an *inference engine*. The *webcrawler* collects pages from the Web, extracts their annotations, and parses them into the internal format of Ontobroker. The *inference engine* takes these facts, together with the terminology and axioms of the ontology, and derives the answers to user queries. To achieve this it has to do a rather complex job. First, it translates Frame Logic into predicate logic and, second, it translates predicate logic into Horn logic via Lloyd-Topor transformations [Lloyd & Topor, 1984]. The translation process is summarized in Fig. 20.

As a result we obtain a normal logic program. Standard techniques from deductive databases can be used to implement the last stage: the bottom-up fixpoint evaluation procedure. Because negation in the clause body is allowed, we have to carefully select an appropriate semantics and evaluation procedure. If the resulting program is stratified, Ontobroker uses simple stratified semantics and evaluates it with a technique called dynamic filtering (see [Kifer & Lozinskii, 1986], [Fensel et al., 1998(b)]), which focuses the inference engine on the relevant parts of a minimal model required to answer the query. Dynamic filtering combines bottom-up and top-down evaluation techniques. The top-down part restricts the set of facts which has to be computed to a subset of the minimal model. *Thus infinite minimal models are also possible, because only this subset has to be finite.*[18] The translation of

---

[18] Syntactical rules that ensure that the subset of minimal model that has to be computed remains finite are described in [Fensel et al., 1998(b)].

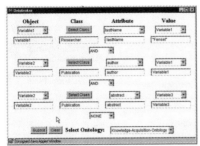

Ontobroker found the following:

V1 = "http://www.aifb.uni–karlsruhe.de/WBS/dfe/index.html"

V2 = "http://www.aifb.uni–karlsruhe.de/WBS/dfe/publications97.html#EEF+97"

V3 = "Building knowledge–based systems from reusable elements is a key factor in their economic development. However, one has to ensure that the assumptions and functionality of the reused building block fit to each other and the specific circumstances of the actual problem and knowledge. We use the Karlsruhe Interactive Verifier (KIV) for this purpose. We show how the verification of conceptual and formal specifications of knowledge–based systems can be done with it. KIV was originally developed for the verification of procedural programs but it fits well for verifying knowledge–based systems. Its specification language is

Researcher **with** *name "Fensel"* **& *Publications* of this** *author* **& their** *abstracts*

based on algebraic specification means for the functional specification of components and dynamic logic for the algorithmic specification. It provides an interactive theorem prover integrated into a sophisticated tool environment supporting aspects like the automatic generation of proof obligations, generation of counter examples, proof management, proof reuse etc. Such a support is essential in making verification of complex specifications feasible. We provide some examples on how to specify and verify tasks, problem–solving methods, and their relationships."

V1 = "http://www.aifb.uni–karlsruhe.de/WBS/dfe/index.html"

V2 = "http://www.aifb.uni–karlsruhe.de/WBS/dfe/publications97.html#FS97"

V3 = "During the last years, a number of formal specification languages for knowledge–based systems have been developed. Characteristic for knowledge–based systems are a complex knowledge base and an inference engine which uses this knowledge to solve a given problem. Specification languages for knowledge–based systems have to cover both aspects: they have to provide means to specify a complex and large amount of knowledge and they have to provide means to specify the dynamic reasoning behaviour of a knowledge–based system. This paper will focus on the second aspect, which is an issue considered to be unsolved. For this purpose, we have surveyed existing approaches in related areas of research. We have taken approaches for the specification of information systems (i.e., Language for Conceptual Modelling and Troll), approaches for the specification of database updates and the dynamics of logic programs (Transaction Logic and Dynamic Database Logic), and the approach of Evolving Algebras. This paper, which is a short version of a longer report, concentrates on the methodology of our comparison and on the...

Fig. 21   The tabular query interface

Frame logic usually results in a logic program with only a limited number of predicates, so the resulting program is often not stratified. In order to deal with non-stratified negation, Ontobroker uses the *well-founded model semantics* [Van Gelder et al., 1991] and computes this semantics with an extension of dynamic filtering.

A hyperbolic presentation of the ontology and a tabular interface improve the accessibility of Ontobroker. Expecting a normal Web user to type queries in a logical language and to browse large formal definitions of ontologies is not very realistic. Therefore, the structure of the query language is exploited to provide a tabular query interface as shown in Figure 21. We also need support for selecting classes and attributes from the ontology. To allow the selection of classes the ontology has to be presented in an appropriate manner. Usually, an ontology can be represented as a large hierarchy of concepts. With regard to the handling of this hierarchy a user has at least two requirements: First, he wants to scan the vicinity of a certain class looking for classes better suitable to formulate a certain query. Second, he needs an overview of the entire hierarchy to allow for a quick and easy navigation from one class in the hierarchy to another class. These requirements are met by a presentation scheme based on hyperbolic geometry [Lamping et al., 1995], where classes in the center are depicted with a large circle and classes at the border of the surrounding circle are only marked with a small circle (see Figure 22). The visualization technique allows rapid navigation to classes far away from the center as well as a closer examination of classes and their vicinity. When a user selects a class from the hyperbolic ontology view, the class name appears in the class field of the tabular interface and the user can select one of the attributes from the attribute choice menu as the preselected class determines the possible attributes. Based on these interfaces Ontobroker automatically derives the query in textual form and presents the result of the query.

4.2.3   On2broker

Ontobroker was presented as a means to improve access to information provided on intranets and in the Internet (see [Fensel et al., 1997]). On2broker (see [Fensel et al., 1999(a)], [Fensel et al., 2000(a)]) is one of the successor systems of Ontobroker. The major new design decisions in On2broker are the clear separation of the query and inference engines and the integration of new Web standards like XML and RDF. Both decisions address two significant complexity problems of Ontobroker: the computational inference effort required for a large number of facts and the human annotation effort necessary for adding semantics to HTML documents.

The overall architecture of On2broker, which includes four basic engines representing different aspects, is provided in Fig. 23.

- The **query engine** receives queries and answers them by checking the content of the databases that were filled by the info agent and the inference engine.

- The **info agent** is responsible for collecting factual knowledge from the Web using various types of meta-annotations, direct annotations like XML and in future also text mining techniques.

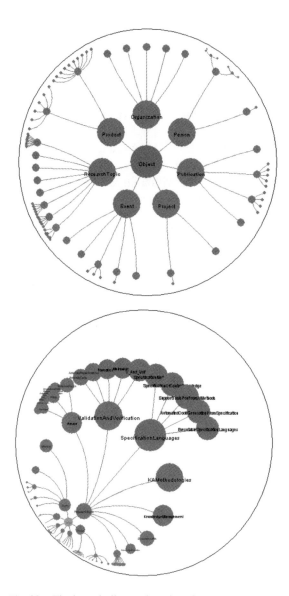

Fig. 22   The hyperbolic ontology interface

- The **inference engine** uses facts and ontologies to derive additional factual knowledge that is only provided implicitly. It frees knowledge providers from the burden of specifying each fact explicitly.

- The **database manager** is the backbone of the entire system. It receives facts from the info agent, exchanges facts as input and output with the inference engine, and provides facts to the query engine.

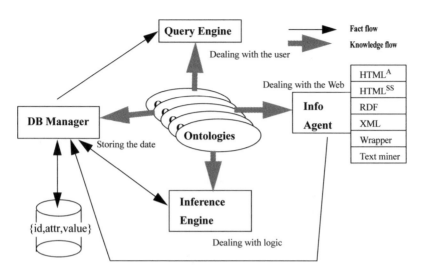

Fig. 23   On2broker architecture

Again, ontologies are the overall structuring principle. The info agent uses them to extract facts, the inference engine to infer facts, the database manager to structure the database, and the query engine to provide help in formulating queries.

4.2.3.1 The Database Manager: Decoupling Inference and Query Response[19]

In the worst case, a query may lead to the evaluation of the entire minimal model of a set of facts and rules. This is a computational hard problem (see [Brewka & Dix, 1999]). In other cases, predicate symbols and constants are used to divide the set of facts into subsets in order to omit those subsets which do not contribute to the answer. This normally reduces the evaluation effort considerably. Ontobroker allows very flexible queries such as "what attributes does a class have". As a consequence, the entire knowledge is represented by only a few predicates, such as the predicate *value* which relates a class c to its attribute *att* and the corresponding attribute value v (*value*(c, *att*, v)). This reification strategy implies that the set of facts is only divided into a few subsets. Using few predicates has the consequence that

---

[19] For the database community On2broker is a kind of data warehouse [Jarke et al., 2002] for data on the Web. Queries are not run on the sources to which On2broker provides access, but on a database into which the source content has been extracted. In addition to the facts that can be found explicitly in the sources, the system also applies rules to derive additional information.

nearly every rule set is not stratified (see [Ullman, 1988]) if negation in rules is allowed. Therefore Ontobroker has to make use of well-founded semantics (see [Van Gelder et al., 1991]) because well-founded model semantics also allows us to evaluate non-stratified rule sets.

Both points, the small number of predicates and the well-founded model semantics, lead to severe efficiency problems. Such an inference approach could only be applied to knowledge bases with less than 100,000 facts. However, it is clear that such an approach need to be applicable to millions of facts in order to be of practical relevance. This pointed out a serious shortcoming of the overall system architecture of Ontobroker. In Ontobroker, the query engine and the inference engine are actually *one* engine. The inference engine receives a query and derives the answer. However, an important decision was already made in the design of Ontobroker when the webcrawler and the inference engine were separated. The webcrawler periodically collects information from the Web and caches it. The inference engine uses this cache when answering queries. The decoupling of inferences and fact collection is done for efficiency reasons. The same strategy is used by search engines on the Web. A query is answered with the help of their indexed cache and not by starting to extract pages from the Web. On2broker refines the architecture of Ontobroker by introducing a second separation: *separating the query and inference engines*. The inference engine works as a demon in the background. It takes facts from a database, infers new facts, and returns these results back into the database. The query engine does not directly interact with the inference engine. Instead it takes facts from the database:

- Whenever inference is a time-critical activity, it can be performed in the background independent of the time required to answer the query.

- Using database techniques for the query interface and its underlying facts provides robust tools that can handle large masses of data.

- It is relatively simple to include things like wild cards, term similarity, and ranking in the query answering mechanism. These can now be directly integrated into the SQL query interface (i.e., in part they are already provided by SQL) and do not require any changes to the much more complex inference engine.

The strict separation of query and inference engines can be weakened for cases where this separation would cause disadvantages. In many cases it may not be necessary to enter the entire minimal model into a database. Many facts are of incidental or no interest when answering a query. The inference engine of On2broker incorporates this in its dynamic filtering strategy which uses the query to focus the inference process (see [Fensel et al., 1998(b)]). You can make use of this strategy when deciding which facts are to be put into the database. Either you limit the queries that can be processed by the system or you replace real entries in the database with a virtual entry representing a query to the inference engine. The latter may necessitate a long delay in answering, which, however, may be acceptable for user agents which collect information from the Web in a background mode. Finally, you can cache the results of queries to speed up the process when such queries reoccur. In many application contexts the full flexibility of the query interface is not as necessary as information answering a set of predefined queries. This also holds for the automatic generation of documents. Here, the document results from a query that is executed when the document is retrieved by a user. Therefore, such a document corresponds to a predefined query.

4.2.3.2 The Info Agent

The info agent extracts factual knowledge from Web sources. We will discuss the four possibilities that are provided by On2broker.

First, On2broker uses Ontobroker's minor extension of HTML called HTML^A to integrate semantic annotations into HTML documents. On2broker uses a webcrawler to collect pages from the Web, extracts their annotations, and parses them into the internal format of On2broker.

Second, you can make use of wrappers for automatically extracting knowledge from Web sources. Annotation is a declarative way to specify the semantics of information sources. A procedural method is to write a program (called a *wrapper*) that extracts factual knowledge from Web sources. Writing wrappers for stable information sources enable the application of On2broker to structured information sources that do not make use of an annotation language to make explicit the semantics of the information sources.

Third, On2broker can make use of RDF annotations (see [Lassila & Swick, 1999]). The info engine of Onto2broker extracts RDF descriptions, and the inference engine of On2broker for RDF is called *SiLRI (Simple Logic–based RDF Interpreter)* [Decker et al., 1998].

The fourth interesting possibility is the increased use of XML. In many cases, the tags defined by a DTD may carry semantics that can be used for information retrieval. For example, assume a DTD that defines a person tag and within it a name and phone number tag.

```
<PERSON>
  <NAME>Richard Benjamins</NAME>
  <PHONE>+3120525-6263</PHONE>
</PERSON>
```

Then the information is directly accessible with its semantics and can be processed later by Ontobroker for query answering. Expressed in Frame Logic, we get:

```
url[NAME ->> "Richard Benjamins"; PHONE ->>+3120525-6263]
: PERSON
```

4.2.4   Conclusions

Ontobroker uses semantic information to guide the query answering process. It provides answers with a well-defined syntax and semantics that can be directly understood and further processed by automatic agents or other software tools. It enables a homogeneous access to information that is physically distributed and heterogeneously represented on the Web and it provides information that is not directly represented as facts on the Web, but which can be derived from other facts and some background knowledge. Still, the range of problems it can be applied to is much broader than information access and identification in semistructured information sources. On2broker is also used to create and maintain such semistructured information sources, i.e. it is a tool for Web site construction and restructuring.

Automatic document generation extracts information from weakly structured text sources and creates new textual sources. Assume distributed publication lists of members of a research group. The publication list for the whole group can automatically be generated by a query to On2broker. A background agent periodically consults On2broker and updates this page. The gist of this application is that it generates semistructured information presentations *from* other semistructured ones. The results of a query to On2broker may be inserted as Java script data structures into the HTML stream of a Web page. This allows the insertion of content into a Web page which is dynamically generated by On2broker.

Maintenance of weakly structured text sources helps to detect in-consistencies among documents and between documents and external sources, i.e., to detect incorrectness. Maintaining intranets of large organizations and companies is becoming a serious business, because such networks already provide several million documents. WebMaster ([van Harmelen & van der Meer, 1999]) has developed a constraint language for formulating integrity constraints for XML documents (e.g., a publication on a page of a member of the group must also be included in the publication list of the entire group). Here the ontology is not used to derive additional facts, but rather to ensure that the provided knowledge is consistent and correct.

4.3   The Ontoprise Tool Suite

Meanwhile a company called *ontoprise*[20] has been set up to develop software products from prototypes developed at the University of Karlsruhe. All tools are already implemented in large customer projects and made mature for company-wide usage. The OntoEdit ontology engineering tool is in widespread use with more than 3000 installations worldwide. In this section, we will describe some of the tools developed there to give an example of a professional tool environment.

Navigating through a (possibly unknown) portal is a rather difficult task in general. Information retrieval may of course help, but it may also be more of a hindrance, because the user may not be acquainted with the conceptualization that underlies the portal. Hence, query and navigating capabilities must be provided and the conceptual background must be made transparent to the user. An essential feature of a community Web portal is the contribution of information from all (or at least many) members of the community. Though they share some common understanding, the pieces of information they may contribute may come in many different (legacy) formats. Hence, one needs a set of methods and tools that may account for the diversity of information sources of potential interest to the community portal. These methods and tools must be able to cope with different syntactic mechanisms and they must be able to integrate different semantic formats based on the common ontology.

The example that we draw from in the rest of this chapter is the $(KA)^2$ portal [Benjamins et al., 1999] introduced earlier. This initiative was conceived for semantic knowledge retrieval from the Web, building on knowledge created in the community. It was built on manual semantic annotation for integration and retrieval of facts from semantically annotated Web pages, which belonged to members of the knowledge acquisition community. Given this basic scenario, which may be easily transferred to other settings for community Web portals, we describe how the tools and technologies support and solve the development of this ontology-based $(KA)^2$ community Web portal (see Figure 24).[21]

---

[20] http://www.ontoprise.de

4.3.1   Architecture

The overall architecture and environment of an ontology-based system is depicted in Figure 25: The backbone of the system consists of the knowledge warehouse, i.e. the data repository, and the OntoBroker system, i.e. the principal inferencing mechanism.

OntoBroker is an inference engine for F-logic. F-logic enables reasoning about the ontology itself, i.e. about classes, subclasses, their relations and attributes, and about instances of classes. It is the server in a client-server architecture and represents the run-time system in ontology-based applications. OntoBroker is implemented in Java and may be accessed by a Java API, by a capsulated socket protocol, and by a Web service interface. The access by a DLL library enables a smooth integration into the Microsoft world. On top of these basic access Web technologies like Jscript, JSP, ASP, PHP are supported. OntoBroker may be configured as a distributed system where different OntoBroker servers collaborate on different computers. A deep integration into databases allows very large sets of facts to be processed. OntoBroker comes with a large set of connectors to other applications like databases, index servers, Web services etc. OntoBroker is also part of OntoEdit which enables ontologies to be tested during development and

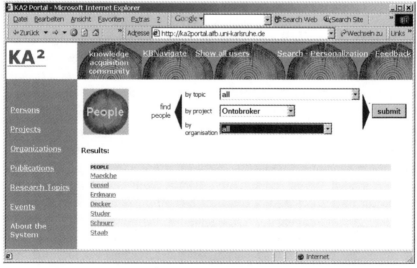

Fig. 24   Screenshot of the (KA)^2 community Web portal

---

[21] http://ka2portal.aifb.uni–karlsruhe.de

provides a smooth integration of the engineering environment with the runtime environment.

OntoEdit is an ontology engineering environment. It is a application that provides a graphical ontology editing environment (which enables inspection, browsing, codification and modification of ontologies and thus supports their development and maintenance) and an extensible architecture for adding new plug-ins. Ontologies may be developed collaboratively on a set of OntoEdit clients. The conceptual model of an ontology is stored internally using a powerful ontology model, which can be mapped onto different, concrete representation languages. Ontologies are stored in relational databases and can be implemented in XML, F-logic, RDF(S), and DAML+OIL.

OntoAnnotate is a semi-automatic annotation tool that enables the collection of knowledge from documents and Web pages, creating a document base including metadata and enriching Web resources or intranets with metadata. It allows to annotate not only static HTML documents, but also MS Word and MS Excel documents. OntoAnnotate uses OntoBroker as a server and thus is smoothly integrated into the OntoBroker/OntoEdit environment.

In the following we give an overview of each module of the tool environment, starting with the ontology engineering workbench OntoEdit, followed by the inference engine OntoBroker and the annotation tool OntoAnnotate.

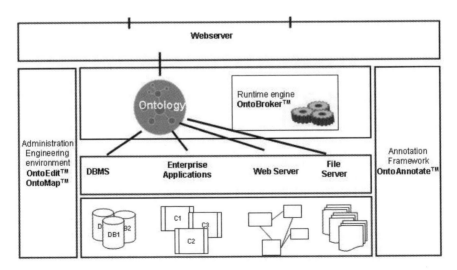

Fig. 25 Tool Architecture

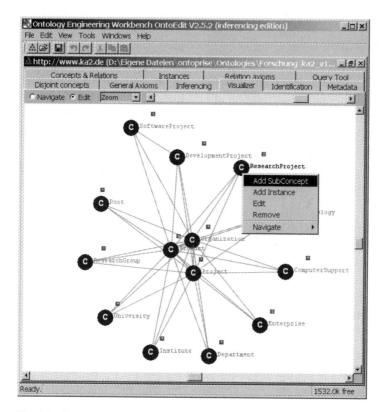

Fig. 26   OntoEdit visualizer

4.3.2   OntoEdit

Similarly to software engineering and as proposed by [Lopez et al., 1999], the development of ontologies is divided into different phases: a requirements specification phase, a refinement phase, and an evaluation phase.

Requirement Specification. You start ontology development by collecting requirements for the envisaged ontology. By nature this task is performed by a team of experts for the domain accompanied by experts for modeling. The outcome of this phase is a document that contains all relevant requirement specifications and a semi-formal ontology description (see Figure 26).

Ontology Refinement. In the ontology refinement phase the semi-formal description of the ontology is extended and completely formalized in order to make it machine-processable. In this phase you can take advantage of the inferencing capabilities of OntoBroker built into OntoEdit.

Reuse in the refinement phase comes in two flavors. First, you may exploit existing structures like existing ontologies or thesauri, e.g. ones that are stored in databases, by semantically integrating them into the target ontology. As in general information integration [Wiederhold, 1997], this involves two steps. The first step concerns the mapping onto a common data model. For this purpose, you can take advantage of the inference engine's capabilities, viz. to read in RDF(S), to connect to relational databases, to provide further built-ins (e.g., for connection to XML repositories). The outcome of this step are data in F-logic structures, but with some rather arbitrary semantics. In the second step, you could build rules to map the outcome of the first step into the desired categories. For instance, you may map a database table-like structure into a target structure of sub- and super-concepts. An example may be given with a database table that contains WordNet hyponyms and synonyms. Our example is based on a locally installed mySQL database system that contains a WordNet database.

1. In the first step we map this table into an equivalent predicate HYPONYM:

```
FORALL C,D HYPONYM(C,D)
<- DBACCESS(hyponym, F('sub', C, 'super',D),
   'mySQL','wordnet', 'localhost').
```

2. In the second step, we define the objects of the predicted hyponym to be subconcepts of Computer if it is known that one of their super-concepts is a subconcept of Computer:

```
FORALL C,D C :: D <- HYPONYM(C,D) AND D :: Computer.
```

Thus, one may easily reuse existing thesauri or database schemas in order to generate a large number of concepts fast.

In addition, you may reuse axiom definitions from a library of ontology modules that are distinguished by a name-space mechanism. A set of axiom definitions specified in one domain is reusable in another domain by the inference engine's capability to store and load axioms from a library to and into different name-spaces in a way that is reusable for another domain.

Besides integrating axioms from a library into the ontology, one may apply axioms in order to enforce constraints on the ontology. We distinguish three major types:

1. **Axioms of F-logic**: These are an integral part of the F-logic definition. However, not all of them are needed for inferencing during the usage of the ontology. For instance, type coercion at the conceptual level:

```
FORALL C,D,E,A, T E :: T <- C[A =>> T] AND
   D :: C[A =>> E].
```

Specify E as a subclass of T if some concept C has an attribute A of type T and a subclass D of C has an attribute A with type E.

2. **Axioms for domain-specific consistency**: These enforce consistency constraints at building time. For example, they may ensure that the domain-specific relation HASPHYSICALPART is without cycles:

    ```
    NONCYCLIC(HASPHYSICALPART).
    FORALL X,R UNDEFINED <- NonCyclic(R) AND X[A ->> X].
    ```
    HASPHYSICALPART is of type NONCYCLIC. Indicate consistency violation if an attribute A is of type NonCyclic and X is related via A to itself.

3. **Axioms enforcing modeling policies**: Such axioms do not add to the semantic description, but they are applied in order to enforce semiotic constraints, e.g., that no subconcept should have more than n subconcepts, that no hierarchy should be deeper than m, or that every attribute symbol should begin with a lower case letter:

    ```
    FORALL A UNDEFINED <-
    EXISTS X, Y X[A =>> Y ] AND NOT regexp('^[a . z]',A).
    ```
    Indicate consistency violation if there is an attribute symbol A between some classes X, Y and it does not match with a string beginning with lower-case alphabetical letters.

The three types of axioms just described are not integrated into the ontology, because once the ontology is fixed and remains unchanged they are not violated anyway. Still, switching them off improves performance, because they need not be revisited and checked again.

The definition of axioms is supported by a graphical form-based interface in OntoEdit (see Figure 27).

Evaluation. The last step in ontology development is about evaluating the formal ontology. For this purpose, the ontology engineer may interactively construct and save instances and axioms into modules. OntoEdit contains a simple instance editor that the ontology engineer can use to create test sets. Another way to get test instances is to fetch them from a database. Our database import creates a (flat) ontology out of the relational scheme of a database. OntoMap is a tool that allows the user to interactively map an ontology to another ontology. The relationships between the mapped ontologies are again formally represented by F-logic axioms. In this way our original ontology may be populated with instances from the the database. If a query is now posed, SQL queries are generated to get the appropriate answers from the database. Figure 28 shows the GUI for the mapping of our two ontologies.

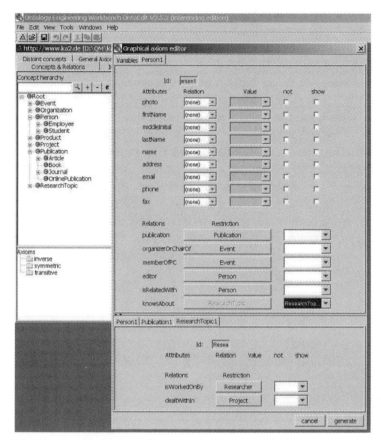

Fig. 27   Graphical axiom editor in OntoEdit

For instance, you may create a test case to evaluate our author rule:

```
FORALL Person1, Publication1
Publication1:Publication [hasAuthor ->> Person1] <->
Person1:Person [hasWritten ->> Publication1].
```

The publications and the persons have been mapped out of the database to our ontology. So it is clear that for each publication and for each person an instance exists. For each publication instance it is known which person instances are authors of the publication. The other way round is defined by our rule. Now the following query should deliver all publications of Rudi Studer though this direction has not been specified explicitly for Rudi Studer:

```
FORALL X,P,T <-
X:Person[name->>"Rudi Studer";
   hasWritten->> P[hasTitle->>T]].
```

In order to locate problems, OntoEdit takes advantage of the inference engine OntoBroker itself, which allows for introspection and also comes with a debugger. Axioms are operationalized by posing queries (e.g., on the test cases specified as seen above). To analyze the results of possible bugs in the rules OntoEdit provides different tools. First, for a given query, the results and their dependencies on existing test instances and intermediate results may be examined by visualizing the proof tree. The proof tree shows graphically which instances or intermediate results are combined by which rules to get the final answers. Thus the inferences drawn may be traced back to the test instances and semantic errors in rules may be discovered. Second, the inference engine may be "observed" during evaluation. As shown in Figure 29 a graphical presentation of the set of axioms as a graph structure indicates which axiom is being evaluated at the moment and also shows which intermediate results have already been created and thus "have flown" in the axiom graph to other axioms. This also gives the user a feeling for how much time is needed to evaluate special rules.

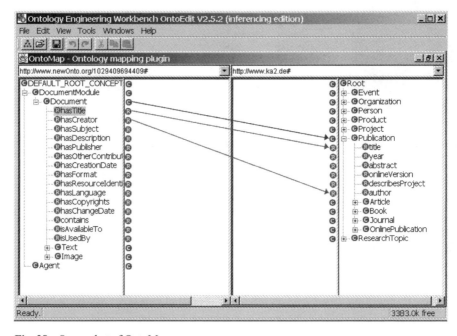

Fig. 28   Screenshot of OntoMap

4.3.3   OntoBroker

In order to provide a clearly defined syntax and semantics for ontologies, the representation of these knowledge models is based on F-logic [Kifer et al., 1995]. OntoBroker infers answers to F-logic queries. In the following we give an overview of the syntax and semantics of F-logic and the operationalization within the OntoBroker system.

4.3.3.1 Syntax

F-logic allows us to describe ontologies, i.e. classes, the hierarchy of classes, their attributes and relationships between classes in an object-oriented style.

4.3.3.2 Semantics

F-logic rules have the expressive power of Horn logic with negation and may be transformed into Horn logic rules. The semantics for a set of F-logic statements is defined by the well-founded semantics [Van Gelder et al., 1991]. This semantics is close to first-order semantics. In contrast to first-order semantics not all possible models are considered but one "most obvious" model is selected as the semantics of a set of rules and facts. It is a three valued logic, i.e. the model consists of a set of true facts, a set of unknown facts, and a set of facts known to be false. In contrast to the stratified semantics the well-founded semantics is also applicable to rules which depend on cycles containing negative rule bodies. Because F-logic is very flexible, during the translation to normal programs such negative cycles often arise.

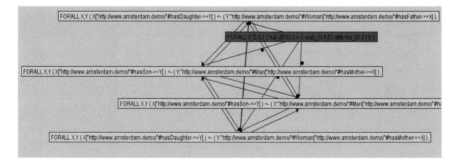

Fig. 29   Visualizing inferencing with OntoBroker in OntoEdit

4.3.3.3 Operationalization

OntoBroker provides means for efficient reasoning with instances and for the capability to express arbitrary powerful rules, e.g. ones that quantify over the set of classes. The most widely published operational semantics for F-logic is the alternating fixpoint procedure [Van Gelder et al., 1991]. This is a forward chaining method which computes the entire model for the set of rules, i.e. the set of true and unknown facts. To answer a query the entire model must be computed (if possible) and the variable substitutions for the query are then derived. In contrast, the inference engine OntoBroker performs a mixture of forward and backward chaining based on the dynamic filtering algorithm [Kifer & Lozinskii, 1986] to compute the (smallest possible) subset of the model for answering the query. In most cases this is much more efficient than the simple evaluation strategy. These techniques stem from the deductive database community and are optimized to deliver all answers instead of one single answer as, for example, resolution does. We have shown this for test cases where all paths in large graphs are computed. The results are shown in Figure 30. We measured the time in milliseconds OntoBroker (versions 3.1 and 3.2) and *SiLRI* (the academic prototype that implements the RDF inference engine of On2broker) need for computing all paths of a certain number of graphs given. In contrast to *SiLRI* OntoBroker has almost a linear growth of time, OntoBroker therefore scales up for such scenarios.

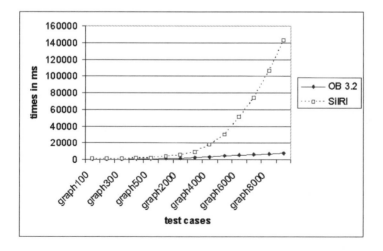

Fig. 30   Comparison of OntoBroker and SiLRI

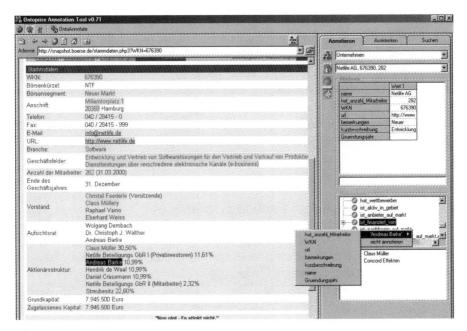

Fig. 31   Screenshot of OntoAnnotate

4.3.4   OntoAnnotate: Meta–Information for Documents

We have seen how one can map structured data sources like relational databases via OntoEdit on a knowledge model and make it processable via OntoBroker.

To disambiguate the meaning of distinct items of information and statements in unstructured documents and make them accessible and interpretable for information systems, these items of information have to be mapped to the knowledge model as well. Annotation is the means to bring metadata into documents to make the meaning of information explicit. OntoAnnotate is a tool framework to create this kind of relational metadata (see Figure 31). It allows the quick annotation of facts within any document by tagging parts of the text and defining its meaning by mapping the text to the appropriate concept in the knowledge model by drag and drop. OntoAnnotate enables the annotation of concepts, their attributes and relations by using the drag and drop methods of the tool. Given an ontology, the annotation process usually starts by tagging one or more phrases in the document. The user marks up the desired word or part of the text in the document, drags the appropriate concept in the ontology and drops it on the marked text. OntoAnnotate embeds the corresponding metadata around the text in the document. After highlighting a part of the text in the document, the user may select a concept, the appropriate existing instance or a new one, and an attribute or a relation. Just by making the desired choices from the concept tree, instance or relational view, the user can quickly annotate the document. With the features of our annotation tool, we support annotators with an interactive graphical means, helping to avoid syntax errors. We support them in choosing the most appropriate concepts for instances and provide an object repository to identify existing instances.

4.4   On-To-Knowledge: Evolving Ontologies
       for Knowledge Management

On-To-Knowledge[22] (see [Fensel et al., 2002(c)], [Davies et al., 2003]) was a project in the 5th European Information Society Technologies (IST) Framework program. It provides improved information access in digital networks. The goal of the On-To-Knowledge project is to support efficient and effective knowledge management. It focuses on acquiring, maintaining, and accessing weakly structured on-line information sources:

- *Acquiring*: Text mining and extraction techniques are applied to extract semantic information from textual material (i.e., to acquire information).

- *Maintaining*: RDF and XML are used for describing the syntax and semantics of semistructured information sources. Tool support enables automatic maintenance and view definitions of this knowledge.

- *Accessing*: Push services and agent technology support users in accessing this knowledge.

For all tasks, ontologies are the key asset in achieving the functionality described. Ontologies are used to annotate unstructured information with structural and semantic information. Ontologies are used to integrate information from various sources and to formulate constraints on their content. Finally, ontologies help to improve user access to this information. Users can define their own personalized view, their user profile, and their information agents in terms of an ontology. On-To-Knowledge develops a three-layered architecture for information access. At the lowest level (the *information level*), weakly structured information sources are processed to extract machine-processable meta-information from them. The intermediate level (the *representation level*) uses this meta-information to provide

---

[22] http://www.ontoknowledge.org

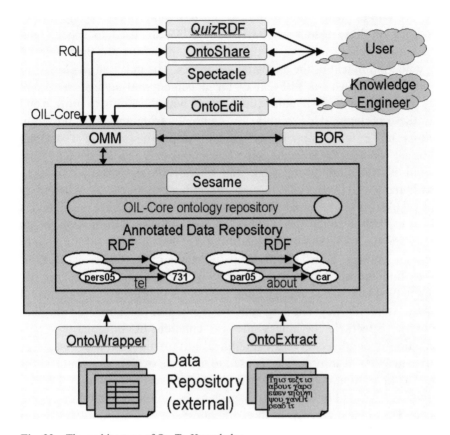

Fig. 32   The architecture of On-To-Knowledge

automatic access, creation, and maintenance of these information sources. The highest level (the *access level*) uses agent-based techniques as well as state-of-the-art querying and visualization techniques that fully employ formal annotations to guide user access of information.

A key deliverable of the On-To-Knowledge project is the resulting software toolset. Several consortium partners are participating in the effort to realize in software the underpinning ideas and theoretical foundations of the project. A major objective of the project is to create intelligent software to support users both in accessing information and in the maintenance, conversion, and acquisition of information sources. Most of the tools presented in Figure 32 are described below.

QuizRDF (see [Davies et al., 2002(a)]) is an ontology-based tool for knowledge discovery which combines traditional keyword querying of

WWW resources with the ability to browse and query against RDF annotations of those resources. RDFS and RDF are used to specify and populate an ontology and the resultant RDF annotations are then indexed along with the full text of the annotated resources. The index allows keyword querying both against the full text of the document and against the literal values occurring in the RDF annotations, along with the ability to browse and query the ontology. This ability to combine searching and browsing behaviors more fully supports a typical information-seeking task than "traditional" search engine technology. The approach is characterized as "low threshold, high ceiling" in the sense that where RDF annotations exist they are exploited for an improved information-seeking experience but where they do not yet exist, a search capability is still available. **OntoShare** (see [Davies et al., 2002(b)]) enables the storage of best practice information in an ontology and the automatic dissemination of new best practice information to relevant co-workers. It also allows users to browse or search the ontology in order to find the most relevant information to the problem that they are dealing with at any given time. The ontology helps to orientate new users and acts as a store for key learning and best practices accumulated through experience. **Spectacle** organizes the presentation of information. This presentation is ontology-driven. Ontological information, such as classes or specific attributes of information, is used to generate exploration contexts for users. An exploration context makes it easier for users to explore a domain. The context is related to certain tasks, such as finding information or buying products. The context consists of three modules:

- content: specific content needed to perform a task;
- navigation: suitable navigation disclosing the information;
- design: applicable design displaying the selected content.

OntoEdit [Sure et al., 2002] makes it possible to inspect, browse, codify and modify ontologies, and thus serves to support the ontology development and maintenance task. Modelling ontologies using OntoEdit involves modelling at a conceptual level, viz. (i) as independently of a concrete representation language as possible, and (ii) using GUIs representing views on conceptual structures (concepts, concept hierarchy, relations, axioms) rather than codifying conceptual structures in ASCII.

The **Ontology Middleware Module (OMM)** can be seen as the key integration component in the On-To-Knowledge technical solution architecture. It supports well-defined application programming interfaces (OMM API) used for access to knowledge and deals with such matters as: ontology versioning, including branching; security (user profiles and groups are used to control the rights for access, modifications, and publishing); meta-information and ontology lookup (support for meta-properties for whole ontologies, as well as for separate concepts and properties); access via a number of protocols.

From a functional point of view, OMM supports the two major scenarios of usage of the On-To-Knowledge tools as follows:

- Knowledge engineering – the versioning system makes OMM/Sesame an ideal environment for collaborative knowledge engineering, enabling a development style similar to that of the source control systems (CVS) provide for software development. The Sesame/OMM plug-in for OntoEdit allows multiple knowledge engineers to use the editor as a front-end, downloading the latest version of the ontology from OMM and uploading their contributions. In order for this scenario to work, OMM silently does smart merging as well as tracking of the changes introduced. At each moment, the updates can be listed and older versions can be retrieved.

- Knowledge use – the access control sub-system of OMM makes possible the definition of fine-grained security policies which can capture fairly complex business logic. This unique feature, combined with easy integration (because of the multi-protocol support for the API), makes OMM an ideal back-end for enterprise knowledge management applications.

- Following the spirit of the On-To-Knowledge toolset, OMM integrates tightly only with the Sesame repository and the OntoEdit editor, but provides guaranteed interoperability with the rest of the tools.

Sesame is a system that allows persistent storage of RDF data and schema information and subsequent online querying of that information. Sesame has been designed with scalability, portability and extensibility in mind. One of the most prominent modules of Sesame is its query engine. This query engine supports a query language called RQL. RQL supports querying of both RDF data (e.g. instances) and schema information (e.g. class hierarchies, domains and ranges of properties). RQL also supports path-expressions through RDF graphs, and can combine data and schema information in one query. **BOR** provides additional reasoning services so as to extend the functionality provided by Sesame. Most of the classical reasoning tasks for description logics are available, including realization and retrieval. The goal was to enable even wider set of applications, such as information extraction and automatic ontology integration. A strategy called pre-reasoning was used to implement workarounds for a number of logical problems proven to be computationally intractable for languages as expressive as OIL.

Information extraction and ontology generation are performed by means of the **CORPORUM** toolset (OntoWrapper and OntoExtract) and are situated in the extraction layer. CORPORUM has two related, though different, tasks: interpretation of natural language texts and extraction of specific information from free text. Whereas CORPORUM tools can perform the former process autonomously, the latter task requires a user who defines business rules for extracting information from tables, (phone) directories, homepages, etc. Although this task is not without its challenges, most effort focuses on the former task, which involves natural language interpretation on a syntactic and lexical level, as well as interpretation of the results of that level (discourse analysis, co-reference and collocation analysis, etc.).

The tool environment has been developed by the companies *AIdministrator*,[23] *BT Labs.*,[24] *Ontotext*,[25] and *CognIT*.[26] It is embedded in a methodology that provides guidelines for introducing knowledge management concepts and tools into enterprises, helping knowledge providers to present their knowledge efficiently and effectively.

---

[23] http://www.aidministrator.nl
[24] http://www.bt.com/innovation/exhibition/knowledge_management
[25] http://www.ontotext.com
[26] http://www.cognit.no

5 Applications

A technology can only be justified by successful applications. Therefore, there is a clear need to talk about the interesting application areas of ontology technology. However, the fast iteration of marketing waves makes it a quite hard to see the real and stable ground. The need for ontologies arises from (electronic) information sharing and reuse. Therefore, we will take the triangle of intranet, Internet, and extranet (see Fig. 33) as our organizing metaphor when talking about application areas. Not all of them are typical of just one network type, however, it helps to reduce the chaos of the overall picture. Let us first characterize the three different types of networks:

- *Intranet*: closed user community, company- or organization-wide use.
- *Internet*: open access; worldwide user community.
- *Extranet*: limited access from the outside (Internet) to an intranet.

Here we classify the following application areas:

- **Knowledge Management** in a technical sense is about the integration of heterogeneous, distributed and mostly semistructured information sources.
- **Web Commerce** is about advanced end-consumer e-commerce (business-to-consumer, or B2C).

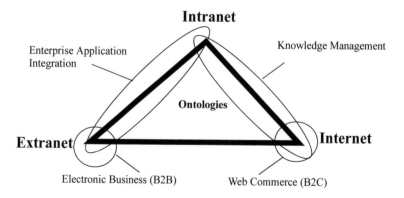

Fig. 33   One technology, various application areas

- **Electronic Business** is about trading relationships between commercial entities (business-to-business, or B2B).

- **Enterprise Application Integration** deals with the problem of data, process, application, and business integration within one or inbetween several organizations.

We will discuss these application areas in the reminder of the chapter.

5.1   Knowledge Management

Currently, the World Wide Web contains around 3 billion static objects providing a broad variety of information sources, and studies estimate that these static pages provide only around 20% of the actual information accessible via the Web (see [Lawrence & Giles, 1998]). Clearly, simple browsing is insufficient as a search technique for this amount of information. Therefore, hundreds of keyword-based search engines have sprung up to support the search for information.[1] Popular examples are: *AltaVista*, *Google*, *Yahoo!*, and *MetaCrawler*.[2]

AltaVista was one of the first keyword-based search engines. Like most other search engines it consists of three components:

- A *webcrawler* downloads documents from the Web.

- An *indexer* extracts key terms from these documents. These are used to represent the retrieved document. A term vector represents the frequency with which a term appears in a document.

- A *query interface* receives query terms which are compared with the database of term vectors.[3] Then, documents which have a similarity factor greater than some threshold are presented successively to the client.

Yahoo! extends this automatic approach through human intervention. A taxonomy of search terms is built up and Web documents are classified in this taxonomy by human readers. This human intervention limits the scope of documents (some authors speak of 200 million indexed documents in the case of *AltaVista* versus 1 million classified documents in the case of *Yahoo!*). Therefore, whenever a search term does not correspond to a category in *Yahoo!* it automatically passes the query onto *AltaVista*.

---

[1] One of the earliest ones is described in [Bowman et al., 1994].
[2] http://www.altavista.com,   http://www.google.com,   http://www.yahoo.com,   http://www.metacrawler.com. See also http://searchenginewatch.com.
[3] In the simplest case, it is the scalar product of the term vector representing the document and the term vector representing the query.

Google differs from AltaVista in the determination of the relevance of documents [Brin & Page, 1998]. Like AltaVista, it selects documents based on the similarity of terms that appear in query and documents. However, the order in which documents are represented is then determined by their quotation index. That is, documents that are quoted often by other documents are viewed as being more important than documents that are quoted seldom. Quotation is counted in terms of hyperlinks that point to a certain document. Given the fact that an average query may retrieve thousands of documents, presenting relevant documents first is much more important than presenting all documents that may be relevant (i.e., *completeness* is often of theoretical importance only).

Finally, *MetaCrawler* [Selberg & Etzioni, 1997] is not a search engine in its own right but rather an interface that integrates several search engines. This meta-search engine transfers a user query to several search engines, integrating and cleaning up their results. In consequence, the user is freed from interacting with several search engines in cases where one search engine alone does not provide the desired results. However, there are severe problems, which will be discussed in the following.

5.1.1   How to Avoid Nonsense
and to Find What You Are Looking For

Imagine that you want to find out about the research of a researcher named *Feather*.[4] Consulting a search engine will result in a huge set of pages containing the keyword *Feather*. Precision (how many of the retrieved documents are relevant) and recall (whether all relevant information has been found) are limited. All pages containing the string *Feather* are returned and many of these pages are completely irrelevant (see Fig. 34). The important page may be missing. In the actual example, we can find the relevant homepage with the search expression *feather+research* (see Fig. 35). However, imagine that he has a heading like "*Topics of interest*" on the page that is imported by a framed homepage. Such a page does not contain any of the assumed keywords. Even if the person's pages are identified, a significant human search effort is required to investigate these pages until the page that contains the required information has been found.[5]

---

[4] The case where his name is *Cook* is best avoided.
[5] These limitations can become somewhat comical. In a recent search AltaVista retrieved a description of Ontobroker as result of the query *feather+research* because this query was used in available on–line publications dealing with Ontobroker (see Fig. 36).

Web Pages   209,035 pages found.

feather - Click here for a list of Internet Keywords related to **feather**

1. Path Of The Feather

The Path of the Feather: A shamanic journey, medicine wheels and spirit animals. The Path of the Feather is about becoming a shaman through your own...
URL: www.pathofthefeather.com/
Last modified on: 16-Mar-2000 - 7K bytes - in English - [Translate]

2. Diplodocus: Light As A Feather?

Advertisement. Diplodocus: Light As A Feather? 156 Million BC 100 Feet 11 Tons. Diplodocus was an enormous dinosaur that grew as long as 100 feet....
URL: www.letsfindout.com/subjects/dinosaurs/rtmdiplo.html
Last modified on: 3-Mar-2000 - 8K bytes - in English - [Translate]

3. One Feather Books and Gifts

Created to preserve and promote Native American Cultures by providing Books,Tapes,CDs,Videos devoted to that goal. ...
URL: www.onefeather.com/
Last modified on: 6-Jul-2000 - 11K bytes - in English (Win-1252) - [Translate]

4. Birds Of A Feather - Home Page

1999 BOAF Show Pictures and Results. Winter Bird Mart Date: Saturday, March 4, 2000 Location: The National Guard Armory, Nashua NH, Daniel Webster...
URL: www.boaf.com/
Last modified on: 18-Jan-2000 - 4K bytes - in English - [Translate]

5. Eagle Feather Data Exchange

Eagle Feather Data Exchange. (EFDX) 611 University Drive Saskatoon, Saskatchewan S7N 3Z1 CANADA. Tel: (306) 249-4747 Fax: (306) 242-9025. E-mail:...
URL: members.home.net/eaglefeatherdata/Index.html
Last modified on: 28-Feb-2000 - 3K bytes - in English - [Translate]

Fig. 34   Searching with *AltaVista* for *feather*

5.1.2   Information Presentation and Access is Limited

The format of a query response is a list of hyperlinks and textual and graphical information that is denoted by them. It requires human browsing and reading to extract the relevant information from these information sources. Remember, we were looking for the subjects of Mr. Feather. We would like a list of research topics like: *World Wide Web, ontologies, knowledge acquisition, software engineering*. However, it requires further human extraction to retrieve this information. This burdens Web users with an additional loss of time. A further consequence is that the outcome of a Web query cannot directly be processed by another software tool, because a human has to extract and represent it in a way that fits some standard representation.

5.1.3   How to Collect Distributed Information

The above mentioned problems are rather trivial compared to queries that refer to the content of several pages. Imagine that you want to find the

1. Joan Feather, Research Associate

Joan Feather, Research Associate. Joan Feather, M.A Research Associate Department of
Community Health and Epidemiology University of Saskatchewan...
URL: www.usask.ca/healthsci/che/feather.html
Last modified on: 13-Feb-2000 - 1K bytes - in English - [Translate]

2. Smithsonian Highlights

Smithsonian Highlights. Special February Exhibits, Events. Exhibition catalogs. Smithsonian
on the Air. Smithsonian Institution Traveling Exhibition...
URL: www.smithsonianmag.com/smithsonian/issue...lite_feb97.html
Last modified on: 13-Apr-2000 - 13K bytes - in English (Win-1252) - [Translate]

3. SC'95 Technical Program

Technical Program. Note: Please refer to the Addendum for changes to the at a glance
schedules below. Conference at a Glance. Daily Schedules at a...
URL: www.sdsc.edu/SC95/techpro.html
Last modified on: 2-Dec-1995 - 3K bytes - in English - [Translate]

4. Martin S. Feather

Martin S. Feather. Philip E. London and Martin S. Feather. Implementing specification
freedoms. Science of Computer Programming, 2(2):91-131,...
URL: theory.lcs.mit.edu/~dmjones/hbp/scp/Auth...hermartins.html
Last modified on: 19-Jan-1999 - 943 bytes - in English - [Translate]

5. What is Recruitment Research?

So, what is research? Research allows you access to anybody you choose, in any city, within
any company. You are not hindered by who is reading what...
URL: www.cors.com/about/whatisrr.htm
Last modified on: 29-Dec-1999 - 8K bytes - in English - [Translate]

Fig. 35   Searching with *AltaVista* for *feather* and *research*

research subjects of a research group. You have to determine whether these
are on a central page or whether each researcher lists them on his own pages.
Then you have to find all the members of this research group and go through
all their pages. The required search effort and lack of recall make such
queries impractical for a large, widely spread, and heterogeneous group of
people (i.e., Web sources). Imagine that you wish to extract the research
topics of all researchers who also work on ontologies. This shows fairly
clearly that the current information access to the WWW cannot handle
information that is scattered over several locations and pages.

5.1.4   How to Collect Implicit Information

Finally, each current retrieval service can only retrieve information that is
presented explicitly on the Web. This sounds trivial, but it significantly limits
query answering capabilities. Imagine that Feather writes on his homepage
that he is working with another researcher, E. Motta, on formal specifications
of problem-solving methods. However, you will not find this information for
E. Motta if he does not repeat the information (with the reverse direction) on
his homepage and you are only consulting his page.

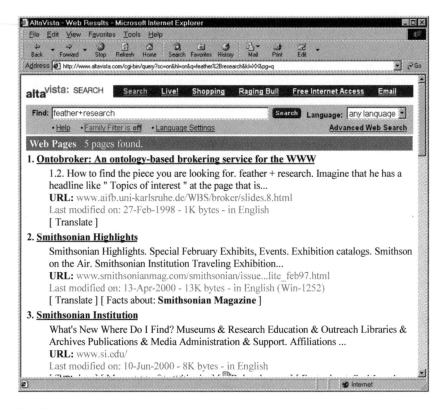

Fig. 36   ... and try it recently

5.1.5   There is a clear Need for Improvements

The competitiveness of companies active in fast-moving markets depends heavily on how they maintain and access their knowledge (i.e., their corporate memory). Most information in modern electronic media is textual, visual, audial, and rather weakly structured. This holds for the Internet but also for the large intranets (often several million pages) of companies and organizations. Finding and maintaining information is a difficult problem in these circumstances. An increasing number of companies are realizing that their company's intranets are valuable repositories of corporate information. However, raw information in large quantities does not by itself solve business problems, exploiting new opportunities, or provide competitive advantage. Information is useless without an understanding of how to apply it effectively. But with the volume of available information increasing rapidly, turning information into useful knowledge has become a major problem.

Knowledge management is concerned with acquiring, maintaining, and accessing the knowledge of an organization. It aims to exploit an organization's intellectual assets for greater productivity and increased competitiveness. Due to globalization and the impact of the Internet, many organizations are increasingly geographically dispersed and organized around virtual teams. Such organizations need knowledge management and organizational memory tools that encourage users to understand each other's changing contextual knowledge and foster collaboration while capturing, presenting, and interpreting the knowledge resources of their organizations.

With the large number of on-line documents, several document management systems have entered the market. However, these systems have severe weaknesses:

- *Searching information*: Existing keyword-based search retrieves irrelevant information due to the different contexts in which a word can be used, or it may miss information where different words are used about the desired content.

- *Extracting information*: Human browsing and reading are currently required to extract relevant information from information sources, as automatic agents lack all common-sense knowledge required to extract such information, and they fail to integrate information spread over different sources.

- *Maintaining* weakly structured text sources is a difficult and time-consuming activity when such sources become large. Keeping such collections consistent, correct, and up to date requires a mechanized representation of semantics and constraints that help to detect anomalies.

- *Automatic document generation* provides adaptive Web sites which enable a dynamic re-configuration according to user profiles or other relevant aspects (cf. [Perkowitz & Etzioni, 1997]). The generation of semistructured information presentations from semistructured data requires a machine-accessible representation of the semantics of these information sources.

Ontology technology allows structural and semantic definitions of documents providing completely new possibilities:

- Intelligent search instead of keyword matching.

- Query answering instead of information retrieval.

- Document exchange between departments via XSL translations.

- Definition of views on documents.

Such systems were described in Chapter 4.

5.2   Web Commerce

Electronic commerce is becoming an important business area, showing strong growth. This is happening for two reasons. First, electronic commerce is extending existing business models. It reduces costs and extends existing distribution channels and may even introduce new methods of distribution. Second, it enables completely new business models or lends them a much greater importance than they had before. What has up to now been a peripheral aspect of a given business may suddenly generate its own important revenue flow. Examples are on-line stores, shopping agents, on-line marketplaces and electronic auction houses.

On-line shops of existing and newly founded enterprises provide new distribution channels with advantages such as: economy of access, overcoming geographical distances, bypassing time limitations in access (like closing hours), anonymity (at least as a psychological fiction), and adaptability to individual customers and customer groups (user profiles and corporative filtering).

The field of Web commerce is still new and growing. Therefore, established taxonomies do not exist. The common goal of the approaches discussed here is to improve the usability of the WWW for electronic commerce by enhancing its accessibility. We will distinguish three types of approaches for better interfaces:

- Intelligent information search agents (i.e., shopping agents) that help customers to find products.

- Intelligent information providers (i.e., on-line stores) that help vendors to present their goods in appropriate manner.

- Intelligent information brokers (i.e., on-line marketplaces) that mediate between buyers and vendors.

Why is there a need for change? Working with the Web is currently done at a very low level which significantly hampers the expected growth of electronic commerce. In particular, it blocks several of the potential advantages of on-line shopping.

- **Individual product search**. By definition, on-line stores make product information available on-line. Therefore, physical and time barriers to the access of this information are eliminated. In principle, it requires only a few mouse clicks to find and access the desired information. However, finding the right on-line store that sells the desired product at a reasonable price may be very time-consuming.

- **Corporative product search.** User profiles that support users in searching for products that are likely to fit to their needs could be built up automatically. Corporate strategies try to find similar users and use their product choices as recommendations. However, such strategies are rarely used currently.

- **Market transparency.** For traditional marketplaces, *complete* product and marketplace information is illusory, i.e., the costs of achieving complete information are much higher than the savings they provide. With on-line shopping, complete market transparency could be achieved. All information is available on-line and could in principle be easily accessed and compared. However, manually visiting numerous on-line stores and extracting and comparing product information is also not practicable.

- **Easy access.** Buying a product is freed from physical and time barriers and the whole process could might be all but automized. In the extreme case, a software agent could search for and buy a product in place of the human client.

- **Negotiation.** Price fixing was introduced at the beginning of the 20th century to lower transaction costs. However, negotiations and auctions help to allocate resources more optimally. Still, the negotiation effort may outweigh the advantages and lead to unreasonably high demands on time (and transaction costs). Automated negotiation agents and auction houses mitigate the argument of high transaction costs and allow optimized resource allocation.

Comparing the current situation with the potential sketched above shows that on-line commerce is far from realizing its future promise. Approaches that take steps towards realizing more of its potential merits will be discussed in the following.

5.2.1   Shopbots

The advantages of on-line stores and the success story of many of them have led to a large number of such shopping sites. The new challenge for the consumer is to find a shop that sells the product he is looking for, to get it in the desired quality, quantity, and time, and to pay as little as possible for it. Achieving these goals via browsing requires significant time and will only cover a small proportion of what is on offer. Very early, *shopbots* [Etzioni,

1997] introduced the first approach for comparison shopping. Shopbots visit several stores, extract product information and present the customer with a instant market overview. "Softbots (software robots) are intelligent agents that use software tools and services on a person's behalf" [Etzioni, 1997]. Shopbots[6] are special-purpose information search, filter, and integration agents[7] providing much better recall and precision than general-purpose search engines, and they usually add some extra service. Their general architecture is shown in Fig. 37. This architecture is based on the concept of providing integrated access to heterogeneous and distributed information sources developed in [Wiederhold, 1992], [Wiederhold, 1997], and [Wiederhold & Genesereth, 1997]. *Wrappers* abstract from syntactical variants in which information is provided by the various sources. The *mediator* accesses these sources (via their wrappers) to answer queries. It has to decide which information source to access, it may decompose into subqueries to several information sources, and it has to integrate the answers. In the case of on-line shopping, the client interacts with the mediator via a Web browser.

In general, three kinds of shopping agents can be distinguished: passive

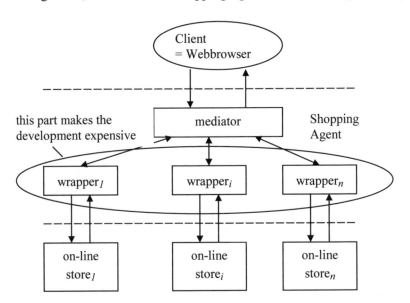

Fig. 37   The architecture of shopbots

shopbots that search for product information based on explicit user input; active shopbots that try to anticipate user requirements and provide suggestions; and finally corporate filtering agents that also try to anticipate user requirements, in this case not only by watching him, but also by watching other users.

An early example of a passive shopbot is *BargainFinder* (see [Krulwich, 1996]). This returns the prices for a CD in different on-line shops in the Web (see Fig. 38 and Fig. 39). BargainFinder allows users to compare prices among eight compact disc sources offered on the Internet. It is a special search engine (in terms of its purpose and sources). It specializes in a small set of information sources (on-line CD stores) and returns price information only. Basically it is a program that automatically queries the CGI scripts of product provider pages (wrapper-aspect) and integrates the results (mediator-aspect). It was developed by Anderson Consulting as a tool for the end consumer market segment of electronic commerce. Various softbots have been developed at the University of Washington (see [Doorenbos et al., 1997], [Etzioni, 1997]). The shopbot is a general framework for customizing special-purpose shopping agents. Machine learning techniques are applied to

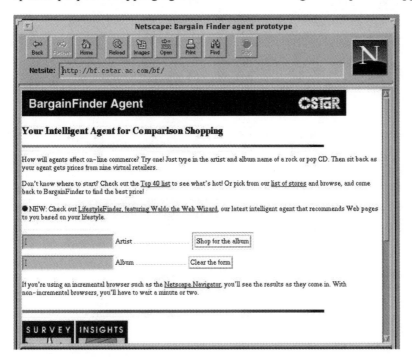

Fig. 38   BargainFinder (http://bf.cstar.ac.com/bf)

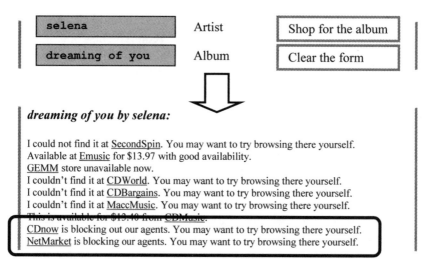

Fig. 39   Response of BargainFinder

vendor sites to semi-mechanize the wrapper generation process (see also [Kushmerick, 1997], [Muslea et al., 1998]). The application of automated procedures for wrapper constructions is possible because many on-line store use similar navigation and layout rules for accessing their sortiment.

A large number of similar companies now exist and we are close to the situation of needing meta-shopping agents that select from the various shopping agents: *Bookblvd,*[8] *Bottom Dollar,*[9] *Buyer's Index,*[10] *CompareNet,*[11] *Deal-pilot,*[12] *Froogle,*[13] *Jango,*[14]. *Junglee,*[15] *MyShop,*[16] *Shop-find,*[17] and *Shopper.* [18]

Originally these shopbots had problems in finding a business model. Web users do not want to pay because they are used to free service. Product providers do not want to fund the agent because of its ability to always find the cheapest source. Product providers would fund the agent if it manipulated the search results. This would eliminate objectivity, however, which is a requirement for high acceptance. Financing by banners requires very high traffic, which is difficult for a shopping agent to achieve. In the end, most of

---

[8] http://www.bookblvd.com
[9] http://www.bottomdollar.com
[10] http://www.buyersindex.com
[11] http://www.compare.net
[12] http://www.dealpilot.com
[13] http://froogle.google.com/froogle/about.html
[14] http://www.jango.com
[15] http://www.junglee.com
[16] http://www.myshop.de
[17] http://www.shopfind.com
[18] http://www.shopper.com

Fig. 40   Jango

them were either bought by Internet portals wanting to add them to their portfolio of features, or by investors who tried to build an Internet portal with them. It is quite natural to view them as a specific feature of search engines.

Current shopbot technology is mostly passive. The user has to play the active part and the shopbot helps to in collect the required information. Active shopbots would search for product information which may be of interest for the user. An example of such an agent in the area of information search is *Letzina* (see [Lieberman, 1998(a)], [Lieberman, 1998b]). Letzina is an information reconnaissance agent. As you are looking at a page, Letzina does an incremental breadth-first search from the current page, previewing the links. It uses an automatically generated user profile to recommend new information sources. Central to all active information agents is that they require knowledge about the preferences of their users. Letzina directly watches the user's behavior and builds a profile from it. This can be achieved in several ways.

Lifestyle Finder (see [Krulwich, 1997])[19] asks the user for his preferences. It recommends documents matching your interests based on your answers to a set of questions. It is a prototype developed by Anderson Consulting. The idea is to take data about the user's likes and dislikes and generate a general profile for him. This profile can be used to retrieve documents matching interests; recommend music, movies, or other similar products; or carry out other tasks in a specialized fashion. A user profile is generated through a dialog with a user (see Fig. 41) and the answers are used to classify them into one of 62 demographic clusters derived from surveys.

Alexa[20] watches all its users and anticipates their preferences. It recommends new additional Web sources "similar" to those currently visited by its user by watching what other users have selected as their next page. It can best be

 Behold! Waldo senses one of these homes resembles your abode. Of course, Waldo could tell you which one is like yours, but Waldo doesn't like to give the store away. So kindly show Waldo in which type of home you live.

Fig. 41 Lifestyle Finder

[19] http://bf.cstar.ac.com/lifestyle
[20] http://www.alexa.com

understood as an intelligent proxy. A normal proxy caches parts of the Web visited by the user. It reduces overload on the net (helping the net provider) and makes off-line browsing possible (helping the user). An "intelligent" proxy caches the pages the user *will* visit. An intelligent proxy is a user agent that collects pages the user is or may be interested in. It needs a user profile and knowledge about Web sources. Alexa is a plug-in for Web browsers that archives and stores all Web sources that are visited by its users. It is a proxy for all Web sources visited by its user community. In that sense it will become a Web archive. It also stores and analyses the Web browsing of its users to recommend interesting Web sources to them. It enables commenting of Web sources and it recommends to the user a set of pages that may be related to the current page he is looking at.

Firefly (see [Shardanand & Maes, 1995]) is a commercial corporate filtering agent. Firefly asks for ratings of specific musical artists, correlates each user with others who share their tastes, and recommends songs or albums which their cohorts have rated highly. It was developed by MIT and sold to Microsoft. Its technology is based on Ringo (see [Shardanand & Maes, 1995]) which uses social filtering techniques to guide users through information sources and product catalogs. It consists mainly of three steps:

- The system maintains a user profile, a record of the user's interests in specific items.

- It compares this profile to the profiles of other users and weights each profile for its degree of similarity with the user's profile.

- Finally, it considers a set of the most similar profiles and uses information contained in them to recommend items to the user.

[Hagel & Singer, 1999] argue that such (social) shopping agents may be an early form of what they call *infomediaries*. These infomediaries are aware of customer's requirements via extensive profiling and help them to find the products they need by means of extensive market survey, and analysis as well as the social filtering techniques they can apply based on their large number of customers. They also help to protect these profiles as property of their users. Because they mediate between buyers and vendors they can provide a twofold service: they can protect buyers from spam and, in cases where buyers allow it, they can provide guided access to potential clients for vendors. They may reshape the business model in many areas of the economy because they will become the portals that mediate customer vendor relationships. They may help to actually realize for clients the total market transparency that is possible with electronically available commercial offers. Also they enable one-to-one marketing for the broader public. As a general perspective [Hagel & Singer, 1999] it is expected that power will shift from vendors to consumers via these infomediaries. Currently, consumers are isolated and generally lack the means to band together. Informediators may become powerful representatives of their clients. Web portals like Accompany[21] are a step in this direction. Here customers come together to form selling groups which enable them to demand large discounts.

Electronic means for Web commerce is based on *wrappers* that need to be written for each on-line store. Such wrappers use a keyword search to find the product information together with assumptions on regularities in the presentation format of stores and text extraction heuristics. This technology has two severe limitations:

- *Effort*: Writing a wrapper for each on-line store is a time-consuming activity and changes of the store cause high maintenance efforts.

- *Quality*: The extracted product information is limited (mostly price information), error-prone and incomplete. For example, a wrapper may extract the direct product price but overlook indirect costs such as shipping charges.

These problems are caused by the fact that most product information is provided in natural language, and automatic text recognition is still a research area with significant unsolved problems. However, the situation will drastically change in the near future when standard representation formalisms for the structure and semantics of data are available. Software agents will then be able to *understand* the product information. Meta-on-line stores can be built with little effort and this technique will also enable complete market transparency in the various dimensions of the diverse product properties. The low-level programming of wrappers based on text extraction and format heuristics will be replaced by ontology mapping rules, which translate different product descriptions in various XML dialects into each other. An ontology describes the various products and can be used to navigate and search automatically for the required information.

5.2.2   Adaptive On-line Stores

Establishing on-line stores has become a routine activity. However, most on-line stores do not employ the full power of the new medium, in particular its *adaptability* and *intelligence*. Shops must be adaptable to general user preferences and his specific current ones give his current contexts. Then they

---

[21] http://www.accompany.com

can make full use of the superiority of the on-line media. Physically rearranging the entire product range of a supermarket for each client and each point in time he visits it is not feasible. For on-line stores this is precisely what can be achieved (see [Perkowitz & Etzioni, 1997], [Perkowitz & Etzioni, 1999]).

Let us look at an example from information presentation: *WebWatcher*[22] (see [Joachims et al., 1997]) is a tour guide agent for the World Wide Web developed at Carnegie Mellon University (CMU). For example, it is used by the CMU School of Computer Science as a tour guide for visitors. First, you have to tell it what information you seek. Then it

- accompanies you from page to page as you browse the Web,
- highlights hyperlinks that may be of interest for you, and
- allows you to provide feedback to it.

WebWatcher recommendations were learned from feedback from earlier users. Basically it learns a function:

```
UserChoice : Page * Goal * Link -> [0,1]
```

where *Page* is the current URL the user is visiting, *Goal* is the information requirement he or she stated in the beginning, and *Link* represents the next URLs recommended by the system if their value for the function *UserChoice* is over some threshold. Similar concepts could be applied to on-line stores adapting them to the specific needs of their customers.

5.2.3   On–line Marketplaces

Up to now, we have discussed intelligent support in finding information (i.e., products) and intelligent support in presenting information (i.e., products). That is, we have discussed direct support for somebody who is searching for a house and direct support for somebody who is trying to sell a house. And what is missing? The person who makes most of the money, the mediator. Take Priceline[23] as an example. This is an auction house for airline tickets in the B2C segment. Customers can place a bid and airline companies can accept it and sell a ticket to the price the customer is offering. *Negotiation* helps to fairly allocate limited resources. Fixed prices are a phenomenon which is only around 100 years old. However, there are impediments to using negotiation.

---

[22] http://www.cs.cmu.edu/People/webwatcher
[23] http://www.priceline.com

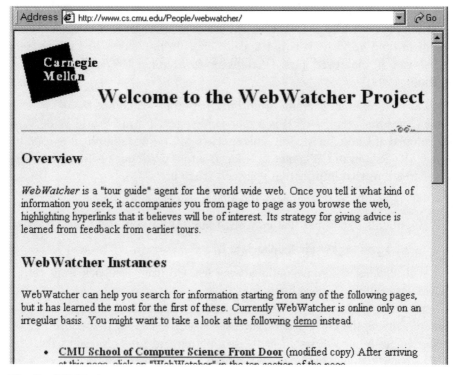

Fig. 42   WebWatcher

- In the physical world, certain types of auctions require all parties to be physically together in, say, an auction house.

- Negotiating may also be too complicated or frustrating for the average consumer.

- Moreover, some negotiation protocols perform over an extended period of time that does not suit impatient or time-constrained consumers.

Therefore, real-world negotiations accrue transaction costs. Most of these impediments to negotiation disappear in the digital world. Instead of human buyers and sellers, agents will meet in virtual houses to negotiate prices.

5.2.4   Outlook

We have described a number of approaches that provide automatic support in electronic commerce ([O'Leary, 1997]). Currently, the mixture of natural language, gifs, and layout information of HTML is the major barrier to the *automatization* of electronic commerce, because the semantics of the information is only understood by human users. Therefore, no real automatic processing of this information can be provided. This significantly hampers the realization of the advantages of electronic commerce. The information service provided by shopping agents is limited: they heuristically extract some information, but they cannot fully understand natural language and the effort needed for developing and maintaining shopping agents is high.

XML will significantly improve the situation because it enables directed information search and the exchange of structured data (e.g., between databases). That said, XML only provides a standardized syntax for exchanging data. Defining the structure and semantics (i.e., the vocabulary and its meaning), is an additional requirement. This is precisely what can be achieved with ontologies (see [Glushko et al., 1999], [Maes et al., 1999]).

5.3   Electronic Business

Electronic commerce between businesses is not a new phenomenon. Initiatives to encourage electronic data exchange between businesses have existed since the sixties. In order to share business transactions both sender and receiver have to agree on a common standard (a protocol for transmitting the content and a language for describing the content). A number of standards arose for this purpose. One of them is the UN initiative *Electronic Data Interchange for Administration, Commerce, and Transport (EDIFACT)* [EDIFACT]. Fig. 43 provides an example of the specification of a business transaction in EDIFACT.

In general, the automization of business transactions has not lived up to the expectations of its supporters. This can be explained by the serious shortcomings of existing approach like EDIFACT. It is a rather procedural and cumbersome standard, making the programming of business transactions expensive, error-prone and hard to maintain. Finally, the exchange of business data via extranets is not integrated with other document exchange processes, i.e., EDIFACT is an isolated standard.

EDIFACT S93A Sample Document
PURCHASE ORDER
UNB+UNOB:1+003897733:01:MFGB–PO+PARTNER ID:ZZ+000101:1050
+00000000000916++ORDERS'
UNH+1+ORDERS:S:93A:UN'
BGM+221+P1M24987E+9'
DTM+4:20000101:102'
FTX+PUR+3++PURCHASE ORDER BEFORE LINE ITEM INSTRUCTIONS'
RFF+CT:123–456'
RFF+CR:1'
NAD+SE+10025392::92++SUPPLIER NAME'
CTA+SR+:STEVE'
NAD+BT+B2::92++COMPAQ COMPUTER CORPORATION+P O BOX 692000
+HOUSTON+TX+77692000+US'
NAD+BY+MFUS::92++COMPAQ COMPUTER CORPORATION'
CTA+PD+:CLARETTA STRICKLAND–FULTON'
NAD+ST+CM6::92++COMPAQ COMPUTER CORPORATION+CCM6 RECEIVING
DOCK:20555 SH 249+HOUSTON+TX+77070+US'
TAX+9+++++++3–00105–5135–3'
CUX+2:USD:9'
PAT+1++1:1:D:45'
PAT+22++1:1:D:30'
PCD+12:2'
TDT+20++++:::AIRBORNE'
LOC+16+COMPAQ DOCK'
TOD+2+NS+:::ORIGIN COLLECT'
LIN+000001++107315–001:BP'
PIA+1+AA:EC+123456:VP'
IMD+F+8+:::PART DESCRIPTION INFORMATION
QTY+21:10000000:PCE'
DTM+2:20000301:102'
FTX+PUR+3++LINE ITEM COMMENTS
PRI+CON:50'
TAX+7++++:::100'
MOA+124:100'
UNS+S'
UNT+29+1'
UNZ+1+000000000000916'

Fig. 43   A purchase order in EDIFACT

Using the infrastructure of the Internet for business exchange will significantly improve this situation. Standard browsers can be used to render business transactions, and these transactions are transparently integrated into other document exchange processes in intranet and Internet environments. However, Web-enabled e-commerce is currently hampered by the fact that HTML does not provide a means for presenting the rich syntax and semantics of data. XML, which is designed to close this gap in current Internet technology, will therefore drastically change the situation (see [Glushko et al., 1999]). B2B communication and data exchange can then be modeled with the same means that are available for the other data exchange processes, transaction specifications can easily be rendered by standard browsers, and maintenance will be cheap (see WebEDI [v. Westarp et al., 1999] and XML/ EDI [Peat & Webber, 1997][24]).

XML provides a standard serialized syntax for defining the structure and semantics of data. However, it does not provide standard data structures and terminologies to describe business processes and exchanged products. Therefore, ontologies have to play two important roles in XML-based electronic commerce:

- *Standard ontologies* have to be developed covering the various business areas. In addition to official standards, on-line marketplaces (Internet portals) may generate de facto standards. If they can attract significant shares of the on-line transactions in a given business area they will create a true standard ontology for this area.

- *Ontology–based translation services* between different data structures in areas where standard ontologies do not exist or where a particular client wishes to use his own terminology and needs translation service from his terminology into the standard. This translation service must cover structural and semantical as well as language differences.

Then ontology-based trading will significantly extend the degree to which data exchange is automated and will create completely new business models in the participating market segments (see [McGuinness, 1999]). Comparing Internet-based electronic commerce in the B2C and B2B areas, one has to admit that the former is more mature. The latter is still being developed; in the long run, however, it will be the more interesting area, as it is expected to account for around 80% of the transaction volume in the future. In general, three situations can be distinguished for B2B electronic commerce (see Fig. 37):

---

[24] http://www.xmledi.com

- **1:1**. Two companies share business transactions electronically. They need to negotiate a joint system and data exchange standard (often EDIFACT and a converter). With new Internet technology this can be done via TCP/IP and XML. These Internet technologies provide better integration with other data exchange processes and tool environments but leave essentially the business models unchanged.

- **1:*N***. One company shares business transactions electronically with a number of other (smaller) companies. Usually it is a large vendor or a large buyer that creates this network. It dictates the joint system and data exchange standard (often EDIFACT and a converter). With Internet technology this can again be done via TCP/IP and XML. Again, a better integration with other data exchange processes and tool environments and a lower threshold for acceptance are achieved without changing the business model. However, an interesting new aspect is the on-line availability of product catalogs.

- ***N:M***. *N* companies exchange business transactions electronically with *M* companies in a *fragmented* market. An Internet-based mediator can help to bring both sides together. It provides instant market overview and offers comparison shopping. *This mediator will significantly change the business model of this market segment. From the business point of view, these marketplaces are the most interesting kind of e–commerce.* Basically, it will replace or at least compete with traditional mediation agents, like wholesale traders.

The Internet and the Web have drastically changed the online availability of data and the amount of information exchanged electronically. Meanwhile, the computer has mutated from a device for computation into an entrance portal to large volumes of information, communication and business transactions. Internet-based electronic commerce provides a much higher level of *openness, flexibility* and *dynamics* that will help to optimize business

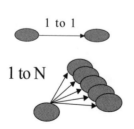

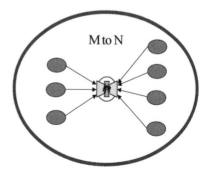

Fig. 44   Electronic Commerce: Three Models

relationships. This type of e-commerce technology may change the way business relationships are established and conducted

- Instead of implementing one link to each supplier, a supplier is linked to a large number of potential customers.

- A supplier or customer can choose between a large number of potential customers and can optimize its business relationships.

- A supplier or customer can change its business relationships in response to new demands from its market.

In a nutshell, Web-enabled e-commerce helps its users to contact a large number of potential clients without running into the problem of implementing a large number of communication channels. However, flexible and open e-commerce can only be enabled if serious problems are overcome. One has to deal with the question of heterogeneity in the description and process standards of the trading partners. Effective and efficient management of different styles of descriptions and processes becomes a key obstacle for this approach.

Web-enabled e-commerce needs to be open to large numbers of suppliers and buyers. Its success is closely related to its ability to mediate a large number of business transactions. Web-enabled e-commerce provides its users with one key advantage: they can communicate with a large number of customers through one communication channel. This open, flexible, and dynamic channel reduces the number of special-purpose communication links for its user community. However, in order to provide this service, there have to be solutions to the significant normalization, mapping, and updating problem for the clients. A successful approach has to deal with various aspects. It has to integrate with various hardware and software platforms and provide a common protocol for information exchange. However, the real problem is the open, heterogeneous and dynamic nature of the content exchanged and the processes that implement the exchange of content. These problems become more serious because of the dynamic nature of e-commerce. New players arise, new standards are proposed, and new products and services enter the marketplace. No static solution can deal with this situation. "Modern" e-commerce needs strong support in three respects to prevent it from being yet another unsuccessful hype in the IT area:

- **Openness** of e-commerce cannot be achieved without standardization. Such a lesson can be learnt from the success of the Web, however, the requirements on standardization are much higher here. We also require standardization of the actual content that is exchanged and business logics that guide this exchange process which goes far beyond the requirement of standardizing protocols and document layouts.

- **Flexibility** of e-commerce cannot be achieved without multi-standard approaches. It is unlikely that there will arise a standard covering all aspect of e-commerce that is acceptable to all vertical markets and cultural contexts, and such a standard would not free us from the need to provide user-specific views on it and the content it represents.

- The **dynamic** of e-commerce requires standards that act as living entities. Products, services, and trading modes are subject to rapid change. An electronic trading device must reflect the dynamic nature of the process it is supposed to support.

Given these requirements there is only one IT technology out there that can promise to provide at least a partial solution. Ontologies possess together two essential properties that help to bring the Web to its full potential:

- Ontologies define formal semantics for information, consequently allowing information processing by a computer.

- Ontologies define real-world semantics, which makes it possible to link machine-processable content with meaning for humans based on consensual terminologies.

The later aspect in particular makes ontology technology interesting. Ontologies must have a *network architecture*, and ontologies must be *dynamic*. That is, ontologies deal with heterogeneity in space and development in time. Ontologies are networks of meaning where, from the very beginning, heterogeneity is an essential requirement. Tools for dealing with conflicting definitions and strong support in interweaving local theories are essential in order to make this technology workable and scalable. Ontologies are used as a means of exchanging meaning between different agents. They can only provide this if they reflect an inter-subject consensus. By definition, they can only be the result of a social process. For this reason, ontologies cannot be understood as a static model. An ontology is as much required for the exchange of meaning as the exchange of meaning may influence and modify an ontology. Consequently, evolving ontologies describe a process rather than a static model. Evolution over time is an essential requirement for useful ontologies. As daily practice constantly changes, ontologies that mediate the information needs of these processes must have strong support in versioning and must be accompanied by process models that help to organize evolving consensus.

Where are the bottlenecks that must be overcome in order to realize such open, flexible, and dynamic e-commerce? Currently, e-commerce is seriously hampered by the lack of standards:

- *Lack of a means for representation and translation:* The Internet standard HTML not provides syntax and semantics for information, and existing standards for electronic commerce, like EDIFACT, are isolated, cumbersome, and costly to implement.

- *Lack of a means for content descriptions (ontologies):* There are no standard product descriptions (catalogs) in the various sub-segments.

In consequence, there is a clear need and a large commercial potential for new standards for data exchange and domain modeling; and for a technology that can deal with the lack of proper standardization.

5.3.1   Means for Representation and Translation

Bringing electronic commerce to its full potential requires a peer-to-peer approach. Anybody must be able to trade and negotiate with anybody else. However, such an open and flexible method for electronic commerce has to deal with many obstacles before it becomes a reality.

- Mechanized support is needed in finding and comparing vendors and what they offer. Currently, nearly all of this work is done manually, which seriously hampers the scalability of electronic commerce. Semantic Web technology can come to the rescue: machine-processable semantics of information enables the mechanization of these tasks.

- Mechanized support is needed in dealing with numerous and heterogeneous data formats. Various "standards" exist for describing products and services, product catalogs and business documents. Ontology technology is required to define such standards better and to map between them. Efficient bridges between different terminologies are essential for openness and scalability.

- Mechanized support is needed in dealing with numerous and heterogeneous business logics. Again, various "standards" exist that define the business logic of a trading partner. Mediation is needed to compensate for these differences, allowing partners to cooperate properly.

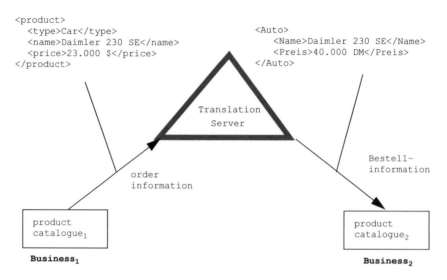

Fig. 45   Translation service

Document integration (see Fig. 45) imposes a number of requirements on the integration technology such as the following:

- The technology must transform the documents at a speed compatible with the databases producing the documents. This limits the usage of logic-based transformation techniques.

- It must allow fast plugging-in of new documents without programming effort as required by XSL.

- Different documents and vocabularies must be aligned via their mediating conceptual models that capture semantic relations between vocabulary concepts and document elements, i.e., the hierarchy of terms and their equivalence.

- The integration model must be driven by a common process modeling ontology and a shared business integration ontology.

Accordingly, to perform the integration we need ontological models for the following integration subtasks:

- Vocabularies that mostly represent sets of terms, sometimes enriched with topology.

- Business documents that mostly represent the part-breakdown of documents into elements and their Ontological models that contain a shallow concept hierarchy but a number of constraints on element values.

- Processes ontologies that contain a limited number of terms corresponding to time points, activities, objects etc., but a rich set of temporal axioms.

All the individual ontologies must be mapped to the mediating ontology that specifies the shared semantics of the concepts used by the integration service.

The business integration technology proposed in [Omelayenko & Fensel, 2001] assumes that XML documents might first be "lifted up" to their RDF data models (the process known as document annotation). Then different private RDF data models are mapped to the shared mediating data model enriched with different constraints and formal specification of shared semantics of the concepts.

An RDF mapping technology (RDFT) is now being developed to represent, reuse, and execute these mappings [Omelayenko et al., 2002]. Specifically, RDFT provides an integration architecture, a mapping meta-ontology that specifies the mapping constructs called bridges, and the technology for map interpretation and translation to XSL.

Concisely, the RDFT architecture assumes that three tasks (vocabulary, document, and process integration) are processed separately. Each specific enterprise must separately align the vocabularies, document formats, and processes with the mediating ontology. The mediating process model guides the whole integration process. Process, document and especially vocabulary maps can be frequently reused, which increases the overall efficiency of the integration.

5.3.2   Means for Content Descriptions

Ontologies provide a shared and common understanding of a domain that can be communicated between people and application systems. Providing shared domain structures becomes essential, and their providers own a key asset in information exchange (comparable to portals in the B2C area). In the B2B sector, ontologies correspond to standardized documents and product catalogs. B2B marketplaces need to be open to large numbers of suppliers and buyers. Their success is closely related to their ability to mediate a large number of business transactions. B2B marketplaces are an intermediate layer for business communications providing their clients with one key advantage: they can communicate with a large number of customers through one communication channel to the marketplace. The marketplaces reduce the number of mappings to their user community from $n*m$ to $n+m$. However, in order to provide this service, they have to solve the problem of significant mapping and normalization for their clients. A successful marketplace has to integrate with various hardware and software platforms and provide a common protocol for information exchange. However, the real problem is the heterogeneity and openness of the content exchanged. There are at least three levels at which this heterogeneity arises: the *content* level, at the level of *product catalog structures*, and the level of *document structures*.

The actual **content** of the information exchanged needs to be modeled. Historically, many different ways to categorize and describe products have evolved. Often vendors have their own way of describing their products. Structuring and standardizing the product descriptions is a significant task in B2B e-commerce, ensuring that different players can actually communicate with each other, allowing customers to find the products they are looking for. This is where *content management* solution providers can provide added value for e-commerce. Basically, they help their vendors to build and introduce an ontology for a certain product domain. A widely used classification scheme in the US is UN/SPSC.[25] The UN/SPSC was created when the United Nations Development Program and Dun & Bradstreet merged their separate commodity classification codes into a single open system. It is now maintained by the Electronic Commerce Code Management Association (ECCMA),[26] which is a not-for-profit membership organization. Basically, UN/SPSC is a hierarchical classification with five levels. Each level contains a two-character numerical value and a textual description of the product category. UN/SPSC is only one classification scheme and it also has serious shortcomings:

- It is not descriptive, i.e. it does not define any attributes for describing the products.

- It is not very intuitive, i.e. neither suppliers nor buyers will find their products in the classification.

- It is very shallow, i.e. it does not provide enough distinctions for a vertical marketplace that offers a large number of products from a certain domain.

---

[25] http://www.un-spsc.net
[26] http://www.eccma.org and http://www.eccma.org/unspsc

UN/SPSC is a typical example of a *horizontal* standard that covers all possible product domains. However, it is not very detailed in any domain. RosettaNet[27] is an example of a *vertical* standard, describing products of the hardware and software industry in detail. Vertical standards describe a certain product domain in more detail than common horizontal ones.

E-commerce is about the electronic exchange of business information in which product descriptions are just one element. The product descriptions are the building blocks of an electronic catalog, together with information about the vendor, the manufacturer, the lead time, etc. Furthermore, a catalog provider needs to include quality control information, such as the version, date and identification number of the catalog. The total composition of these building blocks is what we refer to as the catalog structure. If two electronic catalogs are involved (e.g., when two vendors in one marketplace have different catalog providers, or when two different marketplaces wish to communicate) the structure of these catalogs has to be aligned as well.

One step further in the process, we come to the actual use of the catalog. In the marketplace, a buyer will want to send a purchase order, after picking up the necessary information from the catalog. The vendor has to reply with a confirmation, and the actual buying process begins. In order for the buyer and the vendor to read and process each other's business documents, again a common language is needed. Marketplace software developers like Commerce One[28] developed their structures based on xCBL.[29] This provides a large collection of document structures reflecting different aspects of a trading process. Alining these document structures with other document definitions from, for example, Ariba[30] (cXML[31]) is not certainly a trivial task.

To align different standards, actual business content must be structured and categorized according to these standards. *GoldenBullet* [Ding et al., 2002] is a software system that applies information retrieval and machine learning techniques to this important subtask of content management. *GoldenBullet* helps to mechanize the process of product classification. Finding the right place for a product description in a standard classification system such as UN/SPSC is not at all a trivial task. Each product must be mapped to the corresponding product category in UN/SPSC to create the product catalog. Product classification schemes contain huge number of categories with far from sufficient definitions (e.g., over 15,000 classes for

---

[27] http://www.rosettanet.org
[28] http://www.commerceone.com
[29] http://www.xcbl.org
[30] http://www.ariba.com
[31] http://www.cXML.org

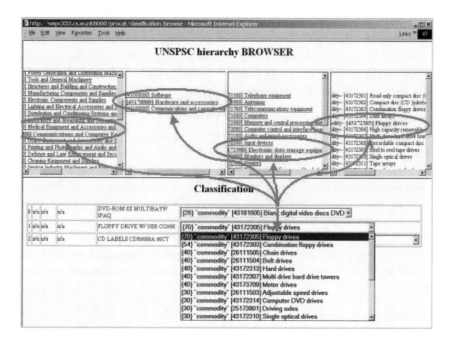

Fig. 46   GoldenBullet

UN/SPSC) and millions of products must be classified according to them. This requires a tremendous amount of work and the product classification stage takes altogether up to 25% of the time spent on content management. Because product classification is so expensive, complicated, time-consuming and error-prone, content management needs support in automation of the product classification process and automatic creation of product classification rules. *GoldenBullet* is a prototype for deploying information retrieval and machine learning methods to classify product description semi-automatically or automatically. Fig. 46 shows the user interface of the classifier. The imported UN/SPSC is browsable from the screen, which directs the end user to the right location of UN/SPSC. The classifier classifies the preprocessed product data and proposes the ranked solutions based on various weighting algorithms. The end user can pull down the proposed list and make the final choice. But when he highlights one of the proposed solutions, the UN/SPSC browse window will show the exact location of it in UN/SPSC with the details of each level.

5.4   Enterprise Application Integration

The integration of data, information, knowledge, processes, applications, and business is becoming more and more important. Therefore, enterprise application integration (EAI) will have soon a major share of the overall expenditure on IT. There are a number of reasons for this trend:

- An increased number of company mergers that require the integration of large-scale software infrastructure.

- An increased investment in existing software and hardware infrastructure does not allow new solutions from scratch. New software solutions have to become integrated with existing legacy software.

- There is no best solution for all purposes. A company may decide to buy a customer relationship management (CRM) solution from vendor X and a enterprise resource planning (ERP) solution from vendor Y.

- The area of IT solutions is fast-moving. New protocols and standards pop up and companies are forced to remain compliant with them.

Therefore, some studies estimate that in the future up to 30% of IT budgets will be spent on enterprise application integration tasks. This may constitute a serious bottleneck to progress in IT issues because most of the resources are spent on integrating existing solutions rather than on developing in new directions.

Up to now, many companies have tended to try to solve their integration needs by ad hoc integration projects; however, ad hoc integration does not scale. At first glance, ad hoc integration works well because it does not require any management and maintenance overheads. However, it is only a working solution when the number of business processes and data sources is small. Only if integration is a side aspect ad hoc treatment work best. When integration needs become serious, ad hoc integration ceases to be a solution to the problem and becomes an additional burden that makes the problem more serious and unsolvable. Ad hoc integrations become pieces that need to be integrated at a later stage of more principled and large-scaled integration projects.

Usually, after a phase of ad hoc integration companies start to search for the silver bullet that may help to solve the growing problem. They are now in the phase were they are willing to buy a global integration platform. However, this is only a piece of the overall solution. For example, a large company has 1000 business processes and 1000 information sources. In the worst case, this would require 1,000,000 ad hoc mappings or alternatively 2000 global integrations. Now, 2000 is considerable less than one million but it is still a number that requires serious investment. Also such a global integration requires time. It may be endangered by always coming too late and never hitting the current state. In consequence, a global integration platform that mediates between all business processes on the one site and all information sources on the other site requires a large-scale investment and a long-term development time which makes it outdated when it is implemented. Business processes have changed during the integration project, reflecting new demands from the market. Applications and data sources have changed, reflecting new IT and business environments. A global integration project will always be behind the development of what it is supposed to integrate. It will only work in a static environment; however, it is precisely the dynamic nature of the environment that creates the need for it.

A successful integration strategy must combine the advantages of ad hoc and global integration strategies. Learning from ad hoc integration means to make sure that we reflect business needs as *the* driving force for the integration process. Learning from global integration means to make sure that we create extensible and reusable integrations. In consequence, we identify three major requirements for successful integration.

Purpose-driven. Let your business needs drive the integration process. We need to identify the major integration needs in terms of business processes and available information sources. We structure our integration efforts around these needs and we employ integration techniques that prevent us from succumbing to the disadvantages of ad hoc integrations, i.e., we care for extensibility and reusability.

Extendable. Use ontologies to prevent ad hoc integration. Use them for publishing the information of data sources and for aligning it with business needs. By using ontologies for making information explicit we ensure that our integration efforts can be extended in response to new and changed business needs. Ontologies provide the controlled terminologies based on structured and well-defined domain theories that ensure the extensibility of realized integration pieces.

Reusable. Use Web service technology to reflect further integration needs based on standardization. Ontologies provide extensible integration solutions. It remains to ensure that our chosen software architecture enables their actual reuse in new business context. Here, Web services as a vendor and platform-independent software integration solution are of critical importance. Web services are organized around the Universal Description, Discovery, and Integration (UDDI),[32] the Web Service Description Language (WSDL),[33] and the Simple Object Access Protocol, (SOAP).[34] UDDI provides a

---

[32] http://www.uddi.org
[33] http://www.wsdl.org

mechanism for clients to find Web services. A UDDI registry is similar to a CORBA[35] trader, or it can be thought of as a domain name service for business applications. WSDL defines services as collections of network endpoints or ports. A port is defined by associating a network address with a binding; a collection of ports defines a service. SOAP is a message layout specification that defines a uniform way of passing XML-encoded data. Publishing applications and their integration as Web services has several advantages: (1) transparency of the specific software environment; (2) transparency of inter- and intra-enterprise integration; and (3) Web services enable the reuse of any integration effort in new and changed contexts.[36]

---

[34] http://www.soap.org
[35] Common Object Request Broker Architecture, http://www.corba.org
[36] A systematic introduction to Web services and their combination with ontologies, i.e., Semantic Web services is beyond the scope of this publication. The interested reader is referred to [Fensel et al., 2002(b)] and additional upcoming publications of the author.

6   Conclusions and Outlook

Currently, computers are changing from single isolated devices to entry points into a worldwide network of information exchange and business transactions. Therefore, support in data, information, and knowledge exchange is becoming the key issue in computer technology. Ontologies provide a shared understanding of a domain that can be communicated between people and heterogeneous application systems. In consequence, they will play a major role in supporting information exchange processes in various areas. Their impact may be as important as the development of programming languages in the seventies and eighties.

This book has discussed the role ontologies will play in knowledge management and in electronic commerce. Both are increasingly important areas that determine the economic success of companies and organizations. Knowledge management is concerned with effective and efficient access to the internal and external knowledge that enables a company to be informed of its environment. Electronic commerce enables new and additional business relationships to be formed by customers and suppliers. Both areas require the integration of heterogeneous and distributed data and information sources. The success of the Internet and the World Wide Web provides the basis for this integration. However, they only provide a necessary not a sufficient condition. Having a telephone connection does not help if both partners do not speak the same language. Ontologies can provide the required translation service. Large industrial groups are working on standards for industrial segments and Internet portals may create de-facto standards. Translation service between these standards enables the various players to communicate. In this book we discussed how ontologies, i.e. formal and consensual domain theories, can provide the ground for this integration and translation processes. We also discussed how new and arising Web standards, such as RDF, XML, and OWL, can be used as an underlying representation language for ontologies.

The use of *The one* ontology for all application contexts will never be possible. Neither will an ontology be suitable for all subjects and domains, nor will such a large and heterogeneous community as the Web community ever agree on a complex ontology for describing all their issues. For example, the Dublin Core community (see [Weibel et al., 1995], [Weibel, 1999]) has been working for years to establish a simple core ontology for adding some meta-information to on-line documents. [Fensel et al., 1997] provide a sketch of the idea of an *ontogroup*. Like a news group, it is based on a group of people brought together by a common interest and some agreement as to how to look at their topic. An ontology can be used by such a group to express this common ground and to annotate their information documents. A broker can make use of these annotations to provide intelligent information access. The ontology describes the competence of the broker, i.e. the area in which it can provide meaningful query response. In consequence, several brokers will come into existence, each covering different areas or different points of views on related areas. Facilitators (i.e., middle agents [Decker et al., 1997]) and softbots [Etzioni, 1997] guide a user through this knowledgeable network superimposed on the current Internet (see [Dao & Perry, 1996], [Sakata et al., 1997]). Therefore, work on *relating and integrating various ontologies* (see [Jannink et al., 1998]) will become an interesting and necessary research enterprise helping to evolve "the Web from a Document Repository to a Knowledge Base" [Guha et al., 1998].

Fig. 47 sketches the Web of the future. Currently, access to the Web is at a level comparable to programming in the sixties. HTML provides text fragments and pointers that allow the user to jump to other information pieces

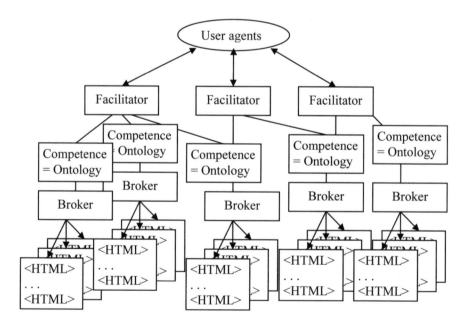

Fig. 47   The knowledge Web in cyberspace

like go-to instructions in assembler programs. The Web of the next generation will have various intermediate information access, extraction, and integration services between the raw information sources and the human user. Brokers will provide advanced access to information sources and describe their competence via ontologies. User agents will access these brokers and will meet the information needs of their human users. Facilitators and matchmakers will guide these user agents and therefore mediate between information sources and information needs. Developing new abstraction layers which enable better service and functionality is one of the key projects in computer science. Currently, we are en-countering this in the area of information access, extraction, exchange, and integration.

Information brokers such as Ontobroker and On-To-Knowledge provide query access to static information sources. IBROW[1] (see [Benjamins et al., 1998], [Fensel & Benjamins, 1998], [Fensel et al., 1999(b)]) was another project under the 5th European IST Framework program. It provided a customizable reasoning service in addition to information access. IBROW developed an Internet-based broker for accessing *dynamic reasoning services* on the Web. This broker can handle Web requests from customers for classes of knowledge systems by accessing libraries of reusable problem-solving methods on the Web, and by *selecting, adapting, configuring,* and *executing* these methods in accordance with the customer's problem and domain. In consequence a user is supported not only in finding information but also in executing the task for which he or she requires such information. IBROW moved work on inference services in the direction of multi-agent systems. Important topics in this area are matchmaking between user requests on the one hand and competence descriptions of available agents on the other, as well as the delegation of tasks to heterogeneous agent societies, see, for example, RETSINA ([Decker et al., 1997], [Sycara et al., 1999]).

Meanwhile the application of ontologies to software components has become a very promising area of research and application. Recent efforts by UDDI,[2] WSDL,[3] and SOAP[4] have tried to lift the Web to a new level of service. Software programs can be accessed and executed via the Web based on the idea of Web services. A service can provide information, e.g. a weather forecast service, or it may have an effect in the real world, e.g. an on-line flight booking service. Web services can significantly increase the Web architecture's potential, by providing a means of automated program communication, discovery of services, etc. Therefore, they are central to the

---

[1]   http://www.ibrow.org
[2]   http://www.uddi.org
[3]   http://www.wsdl.org
[4]   http://www.soap.org

interests of various software developing companies. In a business environment this translates into the automatic cooperation between enterprises. An enterprise wanting to do business with another enterprise can automatically discover and select the appropriate optimal Web services relying on selection policies. They can be invoked automatically and payment processes can be initiated. Any necessary mediation is applied based on data and process ontologies and the automatic translation of their concepts into each other. An example is provide by supply chain relationships where a manufacturer of goods with a short shelf life often has to seek suppliers as well as buyers dynamically. Instead of employees constantly searching for suppliers and buyers the new Web service infrastructure should do this automatically within the defined constraints.

Web services can be accessed and executed via the Web. However, all these service descriptions are based on semi-formal natural language descriptions. Therefore, the human programmer must be kept in the loop, and the scalability as well as economy of Web services are limited. Bringing them to their full potential requires their combination with Semantic Web technology. It will provide mechanization of service identification, configuration, comparison, and combination. *Semantic Web enabled Web services* have the potential to change our lives to a much greater degree than the current Web already has. [Bussler, 2001] identifies the following elements necessary to enable efficient inter-enterprise execution of business relationships: public process description and advertisement; discovery of services; selection of services; composition of services; and delivery, monitoring and contract negotiation.

Without mechanization of these processes, Internet-based e-commerce will not be able to live up to its full potential in economic extensions of trading relationships. Attempts have already been made to apply semantic Web technology to Web services.[5] [Trastour et al., 2001] examine the problem of matchmaking, highlighting the features that a matchmaking service should possess and derive requirements on metadata for description of services from a matchmaking point of view. As part of the DARPA Agent Markup Language program, an ontology of services has been developed, called *DAML–S* [Ankolenkar et al., 2001], that should make it possible to discover, invoke, compose, and monitor Web resources offering particular services and having particular properties. [Ankolenkar et al., 2001] describe the overall structure of the ontology, the service profile for advertising services, and the process model for the detailed description of the operation of services.

---

[5] [Lemahieu, 2001] provides an excellent introduction in these issues.

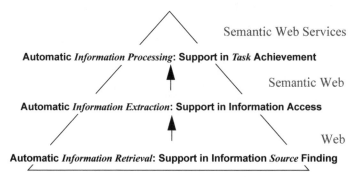

Fig. 48   Three layers of service

The *Web Service Modeling Framework (WSMF)* [Fensel et al., 2002(b)] is pursuing this line of research. It is a fully-fledged modeling framework for describing the various aspects related to Web services. Fully enabled e-commerce based on workable Web services requires a modeling framework that is centered around two complementary principles:

- strong *decoupling* of the various components that realize an e-commerce application;

- a strong *mediation* service enabling anybody to speak with everybody in a scalable manner.

These principles are rolled out in a number of specification elements and an architecture describing their relationships.

Figure 48 sketches the three layers of services we have discussed in this Chapter. Technology like search engines on the Web currently provides support for automatic information retrieval which helps in finding information sources. The remaining tasks of extracting the information and using the information to solve a given task are left to the human user. Semantic Web projects like Ontobroker and On-To-Knowledge add an additional level of service on top by providing automated information extraction support, helping the user with information access and interpretation. Finally, Semantic Web services projects like IBROW also provide a reasoning service that supports users in task fulfillment. Let us take a travel planning task as an example. Current techniques provide a large number of Web pages where information can be found. Intermediate services provide answers to precise questions on traveling connections, specifying locations, dates, and maximum prices. Services like IBROW provide support for the overall configuration of a trip, where several constraints on the combination of different means of travel and domiciles have to be fulfilled. Currently a number of new projects, such as SWWS,[6] are starting in this exciting area of applied computer science.

---

[6] http://swws.semanticweb.org

7   Appendix – Survey Of Standards

This appendix summarizes most of the approaches we have discussed in this book. We have list standards in the areas of ontologies, software, Web languages, text, video and metadata, and electronic commerce. Finally, we mention shopbots, auction houses, and B2B portals.

7.1   Survey Papers

[de Carvalho Moura et al., 1998] review existing metadata standards for indexing on-line information sources. [Hunter & Armstrong, 1999] evaluate and compare several schemes for video metadata representation based on current Web technology. [Manola, 1998] discusses a couple of standards related to developing an object-oriented model for Web documents. [Li, 2000] discusses XML-based industrial standards arising in the area of electronic commerce. [Staudt et al., 1999] discuss and compare several standards for metadata descriptions developed in software engineering, data warehousing, and the Web. Finally, [McEntire et al., 1999] evaluate several representation formalisms that can be used to define ontology exchange languages. This analysis is part of the development activity of XOL.

7.2   Ontology Standards

CommonKADS[1] is the leading methodology to support structured knowledge engineering. It was gradually developed and has been validated by many companies and universities in the context of the European ESPRIT IT Program. **CML (Conceptual Modeling Language)**[2] is a semi-formal notation for the specification of CommonKADS knowledge models, including the specification of ontologies.

Cyc[3] [Lenat & Guha, 1990] started as an approach to formalizing common-sense world knowledge and providing it with a formal and executable semantics. Hundreds of thousands of concepts have since been formalized

---

[1]   http://www.commonkads.uva.nl
[2]   http://www.swi.psy.uva.nl/projects/kads22/cml2doc.html
[3]   http://www.cyc.com

with millions of logical axioms (rules and other assertions), which specify constraints on the individual objects and classes. **CycL** was developed in the Cyc project [Lenat & Guha, 1990] for the purpose of specifying the large common sense ontology that should provide artificial intelligence to computers. Far from having attained this goal, Cyc still provides the world's largest formalized ontology. CycL is a formal language whose syntax is derived from first-order predicate calculus.[4]

DAML+OIL[5] builds on work from the OIL initiatives. It provides modeling primitives commonly found in frame-based languages (such as an asserted subsumption hierarchy and the description or definition of classes through slot fillers) and has a clean and well-defined semantics. DAML+OIL is effectively an alternative presentation syntax for a description logic with an underlying RDFS-based delivery mechanism. The development of DAML+OIL was the responsibility of the Joint US/EU ad hoc Agent Markup Language Committee.[6] Many members of that committee are now part of the WebOnt Committee (see Web standards).

IBROW[7] [Fensel & Benjamins, 1998] was a project that has the goal of developing a broker for accessing *dynamic reasoning services* on the Web. The objective of IBROW was to develop intelligent brokers that are able to distributively configure reusable components into knowledge systems through the Web. Part of IBROW was the development of **UPML** [Fensel et al., 1999(b)] which is a proposal for standardizing the description of reasoning components including their ontologies.

Knowledge Interchange Format (KIF)[8] [Genesereth, 1991] provides a common means of exchanging knowledge between programs with different knowledge representation techniques. It can express first-order logic sentences with some additional second-order capabilities.

OIL[9] unifies three important paradigms provided by different communities: formal semantics and efficient reasoning support as provided by description logics; epistemologically rich modeling primitives as provided by the frame community; and a standard proposal for syntactical exchange notation as provided by the Web community. It was a proposal for a standard ontology language for Web-based applications.

---

[4] http://www.cyc.com/cycl.html
[5] http://www.daml.org/2001/03/daml+oil–index.html
[6] http://www.daml.org/committee
[7] http://ibrow.semanticweb.org
[8] http://logic.stanford.edu/kif/kif.html
[9] http://www.ontoknowledge.org/oil

Open Knowledge Base Connectivity (OKBC)[10] ([Chaudhri et al., 1997], [Chaudhri et al., 1998]) is an API for accessing and modifying multiple, heterogeneous knowledge bases. It is a successor of the **Generic Frame Protocol (GFP)**. Its knowledge model defines a meta-ontology for expressing ontologies in an object-oriented frame-based manner.

OML[11] and **CKML** [Kent, 1999] are a family of languages for ex-pressing ontologies. Translations into RDF and XML and other languages exist.

Ontolingua[12] (see [Gruber, 1993], [Farquhar et al., 1997]) was designed to support the design and specification of ontologies with a clear logical semantics based on KIF. Ontolingua extends KIF with additional syntax to capture intuitive bundling of axioms into definitional forms with Ontological significance and a Frame-Ontology to define object-oriented and frame-language terms.

The **Web Ontology Language (OWL)**[13] is intended to provide a language that can be used to describe the classes and relations between them that are inherent in Web documents and applications. It is a W3C recommendation that will become a predominant ontology language in the Web context.

TOVE[14] [Fox et al., 1993] is an example of a task- and domain-specific ontology. The ontology supports enterprise integration, providing a sharable representation of knowledge.

The **XML-Based Ontology Exchange Language (XOL)** (see [McEntire et al., 1999], [Karp et al., 1999]) was developed in the area of molecular-biology information. The semantics of XOL is based on OKBC-Lite, a simplified version of the knowledge model of OKBC, and its syntax is based on XML.

7.3   Agent Standards

The **Foundation for Intelligent Physical Agents (FIPA)**[15] defines standards for promoting agent-based applications, services, and equipment. As part of its standards it defines an *ontology service* [FIPA 98, part 12] and the way it can be accessed (i.e., the communication aspect). In addition, a meta-

---

[10] http://www.ai.sri.com/~okbc. OKBC has also been chosen by FIPA as an exchange standard for ontologies; see http://www.fipa.org, FIPA 98 Specification, Part 12 Ontology Service (see [FIPA 98, part 12]).
[11] http://www.ontologos.org/OML
[12] http://ontolingua.stanford.edu
[13] http://www.w3.org/2001/sw/WebOnt
[14] http://www.eil.utoronto.ca/tove/toveont.html
[15] http://www.fipa.org

ontology that describes the knowledge types that can be accessed via an ontology service is defined. Here, the knowledge model of OKBC is used to provide an object-oriented representation of knowledge.

KQML or the **Knowledge Query and Manipulation Language**[16] [Finin et al., 1997] is a language and protocol for exchanging information and knowledge. It is part of a larger effort, the ARPA Knowledge Sharing Effort, which is aimed at developing techniques and methodology for building large-scale knowledge bases which are sharable and reusable. KQML is both a message format and a message-handling protocol to support runtime knowledge sharing among agents. KQML can be used as a language for an application program to interact with an intelligent system or for two or more intelligent systems to share knowledge in support of cooperative problem solving. A related approach is the **FIPA'97 Agent Communication Language**[17] (compare [Labrou & Finin, 1995]).

7.4   Software Engineering Standards

See [Staudt et al., 1999] for more details.

The **Case Data Interchange Format (CDIF)** is a software standard for the exchange of metadata between CASE tools. It has been adopted by the ISO and defines the structure and content of metadata.

The **Information Resource Dictionary System (IRDS)** [ISO/IEC, 1990] standard, developed by ISO/IEC, addresses the requirements and architecture of dictionary systems. The four-layered architecture is similar to CDIF and MOF.

Meta Object Facility (MOF) [OMG, 1997], adopted by the Object Management Group (OMG), is a metastandard. It defines a *meta*-metamodel that can be used to define the meta model of other modeling approaches. The main purpose of MOF is to provide a set of CORBA interfaces that can be used to define and manipulate a set of interoperable metamodels. The **XML Metadata Interchange (XMI)** [OMG, 1998] provides rules for transforming MOF-based metamodels into XML DTDs. It therefore provides a general exchange standard between different modeling approaches, using XML for this purpose.

---

[16] http://www.cs.umbc.edu/kqml
[17] http://www.fipa.org

The **Object Data Management Group (ODMG)**[18] defines a standard for storing objects. Its purpose is to ensure the portability of applications across different database management systems. All database management systems provide a data definition language (DDL), that enables the user to define the schema. The **ODMG Object Definition (ODL)**[19] is a database schema definition language extension of the OMG Interface Definition Language (IDL) that describes the standard of an object type and its attributes, relationships and operations.

The **Open Information Model (OIM)** [Microsoft (a)] is a software engineering standard developed by Microsoft and passed to the Meta-Data Coalition which is a group of vendors interested in the definition, implementation, and evaluation of metadata interchange formats. The OIM model suite is a core model of the most commonly used metadata types. In particular, the Knowledge Management Model is of interest in the context of ontology specification. The **XML Interchange Facility (XIF)** [Microsoft (b)] is based on XML and used to exchange OIM models (like XMI does for MOF).

The **Portable Common Tool Environment (PCTE)** [ECMA, 1997] standard from ECMA and ISO/IEC is a repository standard. It provides an object base and various functions to manipulate these objects.

The **Reference Model of Open Distributed Processing (RM–ODP)** [ISO/IEC, 1995(a)] is a metastandard for specifying open, widely spread systems. The RM-ODP provides the framework and enables ODP standards to be developed for specifying components that are mutually consistent and can be combined to build infrastructures matching user requirements.

The **Unified Modeling Language (UML)** [Booch et al., 1999] adopted by the OMG is a software engineering standard. It is a language for specifying, visualizing, constructing, and documenting artifacts of software systems. It is highly compatible with RM-ODP.

7.5   WWW Standards

The **Document Content Description (DCD) for XML**[20] proposes a structural schema facility for specifying rules covering the structure and content of XML documents. The DCD proposal incorporates a subset of the XML-Data Submission and expresses it in a way which is consistent with the Resource Description Framework.

---

[18] http://www.odmg.org
[19] http://www.odmg.org/standard/standardoverview.htm
[20] http://www.w3.org/TR/NOTE–dcd

The **Resource Description Framework (RDF)**[21] (see [Miller, 1998], [Lassila & Swick, 1999]) provides a means for adding semantics to a document without making any assumptions about its structure. RDF is an infrastructure that enables the encoding, exchange, and reuse of structured metadata.

The **Web Ontology Language (OWL)**[22] is intended to provide a language that can be used to describe the classes and relations between them that are inherent in Web documents and applications. It is a W3C recommendation that will become a predominant ontology language in the Web context.

Schema for Object-Oriented XML (SOX)[23] is a schema language (or metagrammar) for defining the syntactic structure and partial semantics of XML document types. As such, SOX is an alternative to XML DTDs and can be used to define the same class of document types (with the exception of external parsed entities). However, SOX extends the language of DTDs by supporting an extensive (and extensible) set of data types, inheritance among element types, name spaces, polymorphic content, embedded documentation, and features to enable robust distributed schema management.

The **eXtendible Markup Language XML**[24] (e.g., [Connolly, 1997]) is a tag-based language for describing tree structures with a linear syntax. It is a successor to SGML, which was developed long ago for describing document structures.

XML Query Languages[25] [QL, 1998] are designed for addressing and filtering the elements and text of XML documents. A standard for these query languages is under development.

The purpose of **XML schema**[26] is to define and describe classes of XML documents by using constructs to constrain and document the meaning, usage and relationships of their constituent parts: data types, elements and their contents, as well as attributes and their values. Schema constructs may also provide for the specification of additional information, such as default values.

XSLT[27] [Clark, 1999] is a language for transforming XML documents into other XML documents. XSLT is designed for use as part of XSL, which is a stylesheet language for XML. In addition to XSLT, XSL includes an XML vocabulary for specifying formatting. XSL specifies the styling of an XML

---

[21] http://www.w3c.org/Metadata
[22] http://www.w3.org/2001/sw/WebOnt
[23] http://www.w3.org/TR/NOTE–SOX
[24] http://www.w3.org/XML
[25] http://www.w3.org/TandS/QL/QL98
[26] http://www.w3.org/TR/xmlschema–1 and http://www.w3.org/TR/xmlschema–2
[27] http://www.w3.org/TR/xslt

document by using XSLT to describe how the document is transformed into another XML document that uses the formatting vocabulary. XSLT can also be used independently of XSL.

The **W3C Web Ontology Working Group**,[28] part of W3C's Semantic Web Activity,[29] will focus on the development of a language to extend the semantic reach of current XML and RDF metadata efforts. The working group will focus on building the ontological layer necessary for developing applications that depend on an understanding of logical content, not just human-readable presentation, and the formal underpinnings thereof.

7.6   Text, Video, and Metadata Standards [Manola, 1998]

Dublin Core[30] is a set of metadata attributes for describing documents in electronic networks.

ISO/IEC 11179 [ISO/IEC, 1995(b)] is a family of standards. It is for the specification and standardization of data element descriptions and semantic content definitions.

The Harvest's **Summary Object Interchange Format (SOIF)** is a syntax for representing and transmitting descriptions of (metadata about) Internet resources as well as other kinds of structured objects.

The **Text Encoding Initiative (TEI)** guidelines enable the encoding of a wide variety of textual phenomena to any desired level of complexity.

The **Warwick Framework** [ISO/IEC, 1995(b)] defines a container architecture for aggregating distinct packages of metadata.

The **Machine Readable Code Record Format (MARC)** is an inter-national standard and is the format most commonly used for academic catalogs. The Library of Congress was responsible for developing the original MARC format in 1965–66. Similar work was in progress in the United Kingdom where the Council of the British National Bibliography set up the BNB MARC project to examine the use of machine-readable data in producing the printed British National Bibliography. In 1968 the MARC II project began as an Anglo-American effort to develop a standard communications format. Despite cooperation, two versions emerged, UKMARC and USMARC, which reflected the respective national cataloging practices and requirements of the BNB and the Library of Congress.

---

[28] http://www.w3.org/2001/sw/WebOnt
[29] http://www.w3.org/2001/sw
[30] http://purl.oclc.org/metadata/dublin_core

The **EAD Document Type Definition (DTD)**[31] is a standard for en-coding archival finding aids using SGML. The standard is maintained in the Network Development and MARC Standards Office of the Library of Congress in partnership with the Society of American Archivists.

The **Multimedia Content Description Interface MPEG-7**[32] will specify a standard set of descriptors that can be used to describe various types of multimedia information. MPEG-7 will also standardize ways to define other descriptors as well as structures (description schemes) for the descriptors and their relationships to allow fast and efficient searching for material which a user is interested in. MPEG-7 will also standardize a language to specify description schemes, i.e. a description definition language (DDL). that is printed on paper.

7.7   Electronic Commerce Standards (Including Web Services)

The **Business Process Execution Language for Web Services (BPEL4WS)**[33] defines a notation for specifying business process behavior based on Web services. Business processes can be described in two ways. Executable business processes model actual behavior of a participant in a business interaction. Business protocols, in contrast, use process descriptions that specify the mutually visible message exchange behavior of each of the parties involved in the protocol, without revealing their internal behavior. BPEL4WS provides a language for the formal specification of business processes and business interaction protocols. By doing so, it extends the Web services interaction model and enables it to support business transactions. It is supported by Microsoft and IBM, merging their earlier proposals XLANG and WSFL.

The **BizTalk framework**[34] is an XML framework for application integration and electronic commerce. It provides XML schemes and a set of tags for defining messages between applications. It has mainly been developed by Microsoft.

The **Business Process Modeling Language (BPML)**[35] [Arkin, 2001] is a metalanguage for the modeling of business processes. BPML provides an abstracted execution model for collaborative and transactional business processes based on the concept of a transactional finite-state machine.

---

[31] http://lcweb.loc.gov/ead
[32] http://mpeg.telecomitalialab.com/standards/mpeg–7/mpeg–7.htm
[33] http://www–106.ibm.com/developerworks/webservices/library/ws–bpel
[34] http://www.biztalk.org
[35] http://www.bpml.org

Common Business Library (CBL)[36] is being developed by Veosystems. It is a public collection of DTDs and modules that can be used to develop XML-based electronic commerce applications.

Commerce XML (cXML)[37] is being developed by Ariba to provide common business objects and the definition of request/response processes based on XML.

ebXML[38] **Business Process Specification Schema BPSS** [Waldt & Drummond], sponsored by UN/CEFACT and OASIS, is a modular suite of specifications that enables enterprises of any size and in any geographical location to conduct business over the Internet. Using ebXML, companies now have a standard method of exchanging business messages, conducting trading relationships, communicating data in common terms and defining and registering business processes.

eCl@ss[39] is a German initiative to create a standard classification of material and services for information exchange between suppliers and their customers. In its core, eCl@ss is an alternative to UN/SPSC. It is currently used by companies like BASF, Bayer, Volkswagen-Audi, and SAP. The eCl@ss classification consists of four levels of concepts (called material classes), coded similarly to UN/SPSC (each level has two digits that distinguish it from the other concepts).

The **Information and Content Exchange protocol (ICE)**[40] is being developed for use by content syndicators and their subscribers. It defines the roles and responsibilities of syndicators and subscribers, defines the format and method of content exchange, and provides support for the management and control of syndication relationships in traditional publishing contexts and in B2B relationships.

The *interoperability of data in e-commerce systems* <indecs> initiative[41] is funded under the European Commission info2000 program embracing multimedia rights clearance. The metadata model promises to provide a semantic and syntactic framework suitable for systems to support workflow, database design, rights management, bibliographic cataloging, data exchange and e-commerce.

---

[36] http://www.xcbl.org
[37] http://www.cXML.org
[38] http://www.ebxml.org
[39] http://www.eclass.de
[40] http://www.w3.org/TR/NOTE–ice
[41] http://www.indecs.org

The **Internet Open Trading Protocol (IOTP)**[42] is defined by the Internet Engineering Task Force (IETF) and mainly deals with electronic payment systems. Security, authentication, and digital signatures are its major concerns.

The **North American Industry Classification System NAICS**[43] was created by the US Census Office in cooperation with the US Economic National Classification Committee, Statistics Canada, and the Instituto Nacional de Estadística, Geografía e Informática in Mexico to describe products and services in general and is used in these countries. NAICS industries are identified by a six-digit code. The international NAICS agreement fixes the first five digits of the code. The sixth digit, where used, identifies subdivisions.

The **Open Applications Group Integration Specification (OAGIS)**[44] is defined by the Open Applications Group (OAG) to integrate business applications. OAGIS defines a vocabulary of business terms and more than ninety different types of business object documents to be exchanged.

The **Open Buying on the Internet (OBI) Consortium**[45] is a non-profit organization dedicated to developing open standards for B2B electronic commerce. It is managed by CommerceNet. With OBI, different B2B purchasing systems can interoperate. It supports multi-vendor requirements, customer-specific catalogs, and secure processing on the Web.

The **Open Catalog Format (OCF)**[46] is the content language of the Open Catalog Protocol, an XML-based software protocol to support the exchange of complex data between product catalogs.

The **Open Financial Exchange (OFX)**[47] is a unified specification for the electronic exchange of financial data between financial institutions, businesses and consumers via the Internet. Created by CheckFree, Intuit, and Microsoft in early 1997, OFX supports a wide range of financial activities, including consumer and small business banking; consumer and small business bill payment; billing and investments, including stocks, bonds, and mutual funds. Other financial services, including financial planning and insurance, will be added in the future and incorporated into the specification.

---

[42] http://www.ietf.org/html.charters/trade-center.html and http://www.otp.org
[43] http://www.naics.org
[44] http://www.openapplications.org
[45] http://www.openbuy.org
[46] http://www.martsoft.com/ocp
[47] http://www.ofx.net

The **Real Estate Transaction Markup Language (RETML)**[48] is an open standard for exchanging real estate transaction information. It was created by the National Association of Realtors.

RosettaNet[49] focuses on building a master dictionary to define properties for products, partners, and business transactions in electronic commerce. This master dictionary, coupled with an established implementation framework (exchange protocols), is used to support the electronic commerce dialog known as the Partner Interface Process (PIP). RosettaNet PIPs create new areas of alignment within the overall EC and IT supplychain's electronic commerce processes, allowing electronic commerce and IT supplychain partners to scale electronic commerce.

SOAP[50] is a message layout specification that defines a uniform way of passing XML-encoded data. Instead of being document-based, automated B2B interaction requires integration of processes. However, although techniques such as DCOM, RMI and CORBA are successful on the local network, they largely fail when transposed to a Web environment. They are rather unwieldy, entail too tight a coupling between components and above all conflict with existing firewall technology. Replacing this by a simple, lightweight RPC-like mechanism is the aim of SOAP. Hence SOAP is basically a technology to allow for "RPC *over the Web*", providing a very simple one-way as well as request/reply mechanism.

The major objective of the **International Joint Semantic Web Services ad hoc Consortium (SWSC)**[51] is to bring current Web technology to its full potential by combining and improving recent trends around the Web, especially Semantic Web and Web service technology.

UDDI[52] provides a mechanism for clients to find Web services. Using a UDDI interface, businesses can dynamically look up as well as discover services provided by external business partners. A UDDI registry is similar to a CORBA trader, or it can be thought of as a domain name service for business applications. A UDDI registry has two kinds of clients: businesses that wish to publish a service description (and its usage interfaces), and clients who wish to obtain service descriptions of a certain kind and bind programmatically to them (using SOAP). UDDI itself is layered over SOAP and assumes that requests and responses are UDDI objects sent around as SOAP messages.

---

[48] http://www.rets–wg.org
[49] http://www.rosettanet.org and http://www.extricity.com
[50] http://www.soap.org
[51] http://swsc.semanticweb.org
[52] http://www.uddi.org

The **UN/SPSC**[53] began as a merger between the United Nations Common Coding System (UNCCS), itself based on the United Nations Common Procurement Code (CPC), and Dun & Bradstreet's Standard Product and Service Codes (SPSC). The UN/SPSC is a hierarchical classification, with five levels. Each level contains a two-character numerical value and a textual description.

WebEDI [v. Westarp et al., 1999] and **XML/EDI**[54] [Peat & Webber, 1997] are initiatives to integrate new Web technology and electronic commerce. Electronic data interchange is being shifted from EDIFACT to better-suited Web standards like XML.

The **Workflow Management Coalition (WfMC)**[55] is a non-profit organization whose aim is the creation of standards for workflow management systems. The WfMC has standardized a language for describing process definitions: the Workflow Process Definition Language (**WPDL**). WPDL provides a formal language for the definition and exchange of a process definition using the objects and attributes defined within a metamodel. The metamodel describes the top level entities contained within a workflow process definition, their relationships and attributes (including some which may be defined for simulation purposes rather than workflow enactment).

The **Web Services Conversation Language (WSCL)**[56] provides a way to model the public processes of a service, thus enabling network services to participate in rich interactions ([Banerji et al., 2001], [Benjamins et al., 1999]). Together, UDDI, WSDL, and WSCL enable developers to implement Web services capable of spontaneously engaging in dynamic and complex inter-enterprise interactions. WSCL has been developed as a complement to WSDL. Whereas the latter specifies how to send messages to a service, it does not state the order in which such messages are allowed to be sent. This issue is addressed in WSCL, which defines legal sequences of document exchange between Web services.

---

[53] http://www.unspsc.org and http://www.eccma.org
[54] http://www.xmledi.com
[55] http://www.wfmc.org
[56] http://www.wscl.org

The **Web Service Description Language (WSDL)**[57] [Christensen et al., 2001] defines services as collections of network endpoints or *ports*. In WSDL the abstract definition of endpoints and messages is separated from their concrete network deployment or data format bindings. This allows the reuse of abstract definitions of messages, which are abstract descriptions of the data being exchanged, and port types, which are abstract collections of operations. The concrete protocol and data format specifications for a particular port type constitute a binding. A port is defined by associating a network address with a binding; a collection of ports define a service.

The **Web Services Flow Language (WSFL)**[58] [Leymann, 2001] is an XML language for the description of compositions of Web services. WSFL considers two types of compositions: the first type specifies the appropriate usage pattern of a collection of Web services, in such a way that the resulting composition describes how to achieve a particular business goal; typically, the result is a description of a business process. The second type specifies the interaction pattern of a collection of Web services; in this case, the result is a description of the overall partner interactions. WSFL is very close in spirit to WSMF, but lacks some of the important modeling features of the latter. Examples are the difference between private and publically visible business logic as well as the use of ontologies to keep descriptions reusable. Still, a WSMF-conforming language could be defined as an extension of WSFL.

The **Web Service Inspection Language (WSIL)**[59] specification provides an XML format for assisting in the inspection of a site for available services and a set of rules for how inspection-related information should be made available for consumption (see [Ballinger et al., 2001]).

The **Web Service Modeling Framework (WSMF)**[60] provides the appropriate conceptual model for developing and describing Web services and their composition. The philosophy of WSMF is based on the principle of maximal decoupling complemented by scalable mediation service. This is a prerequisite for applying Semantic Web technology for Web service discovery, configuration, comparison, and combination. A model in WSMF consists of four main elements: ontologies that provide the terminology used by other elements; goal repositories that define the problems that should be solved by Web services; Web service descriptions that define various aspects of a Web service; and mediators which bypass interoperability problems.

---

[57] http://www.wsdl.org
[58] http://www.wsfl.org
[59] http://www.wsil.org
[60] http://swws.semanticweb.org

Automation of business processes based on Web services requires a notation for the specification of message exchange behavior among participating Web services. **XLANG**[61] [Thatte, 2001] is proposed to serve as the basis for automated protocol engines that can track the state of process instances and help enforce protocol correctness in message flows.

---

[61] http://www.xlang.org

References

[Amann & Fundulaki, 1999]
   B. Amann and I. Fundulaki: Integrating Ontologies and thesauri to build RDF schemas. Third European Conference on Research and Advanced Technology for Digital Libraries (ECDL '99), Paris, France, September 22–24, 1999.

[Ankolenkar et al., 2001]
   A. Ankolenkar, M. Burstein, J. R. Hobbs, O. Lassila, D. L. Martin, D. McDermott, S. A. McIlraith, S. Narayanan, M. Paolucci, T. R. Payne and K. Sycara: DAML-S: Web Service Description for the Semantic Web. In I. Horrocks and J. Hendler (eds.), *The Semantic Web – ISWC 2002, First International Semantic Web Conference*, Sardinia, Italy, June 9–12, 2002., Lecture Notes in Computer Science (LNCS 2342), Springer 2002.

[Arkin, 2001]
   A. Arkin: Business Process Modeling Language (BPML), Working Draft 0.4, 2001. http://www.bpmi.org.

[Baader et al., 1991]
   F. Baader, H.-J. Bürckert, J. Heinsohn, J. Müller, B. Hollunder, B. Nebel, W. Nutt, and H.-J. Profitlich: Terminological Knowledge Representation: A Proposal for a Terminological Logic. DFKI Technical Memo TM-90-04, Deutsches Forschungszentrum für Künstliche Intelligenz, Kaiserslautern, Germany, 1990. Updated version, taking into account the results of a discussion at the International Worksop on Terminological Logics, Dagstuhl, May 1991.

[Ballinger et al., 2001]
   K. Ballinger, P. Brittenham, A. Malhotra, W. A. Nagy, and S. Pharies: Web Services Inspection Language (WS-Inspection) 1.0. http://www-106.ibm.com/developerworks/webservices/library/ws-wsilspec.html, 2001.

[Banerji et al., 2001]
   A. Banerji, C. Bartolini, D. Beringer, V. Chopella, K. Govindarajan, A. Karp, H. Kuno, M. Lemon, G. Pogossiants, S. Sharma, S. Williams: Web Services Conversation Language (WSCL), HP white paper, 2001.

[Benjamins et al., 1998]
   V. R. Benjamins, E. Plaza, E. Motta, D. Fensel, R. Studer, B. Wielinga, G. Schreiber, Z. Zdrahal, and S. Decker: An intelligent brokering service for knowledge-component reuse on the world wide web. In *Proceedings of the 11th Banff Knowledge Acquisition for Knowledge-Based Systems Workshop (KAW98)*, Banff, Canada, April 18–23, 1998.

[Benjamins et al., 1999]
   V. R. Benjamins, D. Fensel, S. Decker, and A. Gomez Perez: (KA)[2]: Building Ontologies for the Internet: a Mid Term Report, *International Journal of Human-Computer Studies*, 51:687–712, 1999.

[Benjamins et al., 1999]
   D. Beringer, H. Kuno, and M. Lemon: Using WSCL in a UDDI Registry 1.02, UDDI Working Draft Technical Note Document, May 5, 2001. http://www.uddi.org/pubs/wscl_TN_forUDDI_5_16_011.doc.

[Biron & Malhotra, 2000]
   P. V. Biron and A. Malhotra: XML Schema Part 2: data types, Candidate

Recommendation, 24 October 2000.
http://www.w3.org/TR/2000/CR-xmlschema-2-20001024

[Booch et al., 1999]
G. Booch, J. Rumbaugh, and I. Jacobson: *The Unified Modeling Language User Guide*, Addison-Wesley, 1999.

[Borgida et al., 1989]
A. Borgida, R. J. Brachman, D. L. McGuinness, and L. A. Resnick: CLASSIC: A structural data model for objects. In *Proceedings of the 1989 ACM SIGMOD International Conference on Mangement of Data*, pp. 59–67, 1989.

[Borgida & Patel-Schneider, 1994]
A. Borgida and P. F. Patel-Schneider: A Semantics and Complete Algorithm for Subsumption in the CLASSIC Description Logic, *Journal of Artificial Intelligence Reserach*, 1:277–308, 1994.

[Borst & Akkermans, 1997]
W. N. Borst and J. M. Akkermans: Engineering Ontologies, *International Journal of Human-Computer Studies*, 46(2/3):365–406, 1997.

[Bowman et al., 1994]
C. M. Bowman, P. B. Danzig, U. Manber, and M. F. Schwartz: Scalable Internet Resource Discovery: Research Problems and Approaches, *Communications of the ACM*, 37(8):98–107, August 1994.

[Brachman & Schmolze, 1985]
R. Brachman and J. Schmolze: An Overview of the KL–ONE Knowledge Representation System, *Cognitive Science*, 9(2):171–216, 1985.

[Brewka & Dix, 1999]
G. Brewka and J. Dix: Knowledge Representation with Logic Programs. In D. Gabbay et al. (eds.), *Handbook of Philosophical Logic* (2nd ed.), Vol 6, *Methodologies*, Reidel, 1999.

[Brickley et al., 1998]
D. Brickley, R. Guha, and A. Layman (eds.): *Resource Description Framework (RDF) Schema Specification*. W3C Working Draft, August 1998.
http://www.w3c.org/TR/WD-rdf-schema.

[Brin & Page, 1998]
S. Brin and L. Page: The anatomy of a large-scale hypertextual web search engine. In *Proceedings of the 7th International World Wide Web Conference (WWW-7)*, Brisbane, Australia, April 14–18, 1998.

[Broekstra et al., 2000]
J. Broekstra, C. Fluit, and F. van Harmelen: The State of the Art on Representation and Query Languages for Semistructured Data. Project deliverable 8, EU-IST On-To-Knowledge IST-1999-10132, 2000. http://www.ontoknowledge.org/downl/del8.pdf

[Bussler, 2001]
C. Bussler: The role of B2B protocols in inter–enterprise process execution. In *Proceedings of Workshop on Technologies for E-Services (TES 2001) (in cooperation with VLDB2001)*, Rome, Italy, September 2001.

[Calvanese et al., 1995]
D. Calvanese, G. De Giacomo, and M. Lenzerini: Structured objects: Modeling and reasoning. In *Proceedings of the Fourth International Conference on Deductive and Object-Oriented Databases (DOOD-95)*, Lecture Notes in Computer Science (LNCS 1013), Springer, 1995.

[Chalupsky, 2000]
H. Chalupsky: OntoMorph: A translation system for symbolic logic. In A. G. Cohn, F. Giunchiglia, and B. Selman (eds.): *KR2000: Principles of Knowledge Representation and Reasoning*, pp. 471–482, Morgan Kaufmann, 2000.

[Chaudhri et al., 1997]
V. K. Chaudhri, A. Farquhar, R. Fikes, P. D. Karp, and J. P. Rice: *Open Knowledge Base Connectivity 2.0.*, Technical Report KSL-98-06, Knowledge Systems Laboratory, Stanford, July 1997.

[Chaudhri et al., 1998]
V. K. Chaudhri, A. Farquhar, R. Fikes, P. D. Karp, and J. P. Rice: OKBC: A foundation for knowledge base interoperability. In *Proceedings of the National Conference on Artificial Intelligence (AAAI98)*, pp. 600–607, July 1998.

[Christensen et al., 2001]
E. Christensen, F. Curbera, G. Meredith, S. Weerawarana: Web Services Description Language (WSDL) 1.1, March 2001. http://www.w3.org/TR/wsdl.

[Clark, 1999]
J. Clark: XSL Transformations (XSLT) Version 1.0, W3C Working Draft, August 1999. See http://www.w3.org/TR/WD-xslt.

[Connolly, 1997]
D. Connolly: *XML: Principles, Tools, and Techniques*, O'Reilly, 1997.

[Cranefield & Purvis, 1999]
S. Cranefield and M. Purvis: UML as an ontology modelling language. In *Proceedings of the IJCAI-99 Workshop on Intelligent Information Integration*, July 31, 1999 in conjunction with the Sixteenth International Joint Conference on Artificial Intelligence, Stockholm, Sweden.

[de Carvalho Moura et al., 1998]
A. M. de Carvalho Moura, M. L. Machado Campos, and C. M. Barreto: A survey on metadata for describing and retrieving Internet resources, *World Wide Web*, 1:221–240, 1998.

[Dao & Perry, 1996]
S. Dao and B. Perry: Information Mediation in Cyberspace: Scalable Methods for Declarative Information Networks, *Journal of Intelligent Information Systems*, 6(2/3), 1996.

[Davies et al., 2002(a)]
J. Davies, U. Krohn, and R. Weeks: QuizRDF: search technology for the semantic web. In WWW2002 workshop on RDF & Semantic Web Applications, 11th International WWW Conference WWW2002, Hawaii, USA, 2002.

[Davies et al., 2002(b)]
J. Davies, A. Duke, and A. Stonkus: OntoShare: Using Ontologies for Knowledge Sharing. In WWW2002 workshop on RDF & Semantic Web Applications, 11th International WWW Conference WWW2002, Hawaii, USA, 2002.

[Davies et al., 2003]
J. Davies, D. Fensel, and F. van Harmelen (eds.): *Towards the Semantic Web: Ontology-Driven Knowledge Management*, John Wiley & Sons, 2003.

[Dean et al., 2002]
M. Dean, D. Connolly, F. van Harmelen, J. Hendler, I. Horrocks, D. L. McGuinness, P. F. Patel-Schneider, and L. A. Stein: Web Ontology Language (OWL) Reference Version 1.0, W3C Working Draft 12 November 2002, http://www.w3.org/TR/owl-ref/.

[De Giacomo & Lenzerini, 1995]
G. De Giacomo and M. Lenzerini: What's in an aggregate: foundations for description logics with tupels and sets. In *Proceedings of the 14th International Conference on Artificial Intelligence (IJCAI-95)*, Montreal, Canada, 1995.

[Decker et al., 1997]
K. Decker, K. Sycara, and M. Williamson: Middle-Agents for the Internet. In *Proceedings of the 15th International Joint Conference on AI (IJCAI97)*, Nagoya, Japan, August 23–29, 1997.

[Decker et al., 1998]
S. Decker, D. Brickley, J. Saarela, and J. Angele: A query service for RDF. In [QL, 1998].

[Decker et al., 1999]
S. Decker, M. Erdmann, D. Fensel, and R. Studer: Ontobroker: Ontology based Access to Distributed and Semi-Structured Information. In R. Meersman et al. (eds.), *Semantic Issues in Multimedia Systems*, Kluwer Academic, 1999.

[Ding et al., 2002]
Y. Ding, M. Korotkiy, B. Omelayenko, V. Kartseva, V. Zykov, M. Klein, E. Schulten, and D. Fensel: GoldenBullet in a nutshell. In *Proceedings of the 15th Internation FLAIRS Conference*, Pensacola, Florida, May 2002.

[Doorenbos et al., 1997]
R. B. Doorenbos, O. Etzioni, and D. S. Weld: A scalable comparison-shopping agent for the world-wide web. In *Proceedings of the AGENTS 97 Conference*, 1997. http://www.cs.washington.edu/research/shopbot.

[ECMA, 1997]
European Computer Manufactur's Association (ECMA): *Portable Common Tool Environment (PCTE)–Mapping from CASE Data Interchange Format (CDIF) to PCTE*, 1997.
http://www.ecma.ch/stand/Ecma-270.htm.

[EDIFACT]
United Nation: *UN/EDIFACT-Directory*. http://www.unece.org/trade/untdid, 1999.

[Erdmann & Studer, 1999]
M. Erdmann and R. Studer: *Ontologies as conceptual models for XML documents*, Research Report, Institute AIFB, University of Karlsruhe,Germany, 1999.

[Erdmann & Studer, 2001]
M. Erdmann and R. Studer: How to structure and access XML documents with ontologies, *Data and Knowledge Engineering*, 36(3), 2001.

[Erikson et al., 1999]
H. Erikson, R. W. Fergerson, Y. Shahar, and M. A. Musen: Automated generation of ontology editors. In *Proceedings of the Twelfth Workshop on Knowledge Acquisition, Modeling and Management (KAW99)*, Banff, Alberta, Canada, October 16–21, 1999.

[Etzioni, 1997]
O. Etzioni: Moving Up the Information Food Chain, *AI Magazine*, 18(2), 1997.

[Fallside, 2000]
D. C. Fallside: XML Schema Part 0: Primer, Candidate Recommendation. October 2000. http://www.w3.org/TR/2000/CR-xmlschema-0-20001024.

[Farquhar et al., 1997]
A. Farquhar, R. Fikes, and J. Rice, The Ontolingua Server: A Tool for Collaborative Ontology Construction, *International Journal of Human–Computer Studies*, 46:707–728, 1997.

[Fellbaum, 1999]
C. Fellbaum (ed.): *WordNet: An Electronic Lexical Database*, MIT Press, 1999.

[Fensel & Benjamins, 1998]
D. Fensel and V. R. Benjamins: Key issues for automated problem-solving methods reuse. In *Proceedings of the 13th European Conference on Artificial Intelligence (ECAI–98)*, Brighton, UK, August 1998, pp. 63–67.

[Fensel & Groenboom, 1997]
D. Fensel and R. Groenboom: Specifying knowledge–based systems with reusable components. In *Proceedings of the 9th International Conference on Software Engineering and Knowledge Engineering (SEKE '97)*, Madrid, 1997.

[Fensel et al., 1997]
D. Fensel, M. Erdmann, and R. Studer: Ontology groups: semantically enriched subnets

of the WWW. In *Proceedings of the 1st International Workshop on Intelligent Information Integration during the 21st German Annual Conference on Artificial Intelligence*, Freiburg, Germany, September 9–12, 1997.

[Fensel et al., 1998(a)]
D. Fensel, S. Decker, M. Erdmann, and R. Studer: Ontobroker: The very high idea. In *Proceedings of the 11th International Flairs Conference (FLAIRS-98)*, Sanibal Island, Florida, USA, pp. 131–135, May 1998.

[Fensel et al., 1998(b)]
D. Fensel, J. Angele, and R. Studer: The Knowledge Acquisition and Representation Language KARL, *IEEE Transactions on Knowledge and Data Engineering*, 10(4):527–550, 1998.

[Fensel et al., 1999(a)]
D. Fensel, J. Angele, S. Decker, M. Erdmann, H.-P. Schnurr, S. Staab, R. Studer, and A. Witt: On2broker: Semantic-based access to information sources at the WWW. In *Proceedings of the World Conference on the WWW and Internet (WebNet 99)*, Honolulu, Hawaii, USA, October 25–30, 1999.

[Fensel et al., 1999(b)]
D. Fensel, V. R. Benjamins, E. Motta, and B. Wielinga: UPML: A framework for knowledge system reuse. In *Proceedings of the International Joint Conference on AI (IJCAI–99)*, Stockholm, Sweden, July 31–August 5, 1999.

[Fensel et al., 2000(a)]
D. Fensel, S. Decker, M. Erdmann, H.-P. Schnurr, R. Studer, and A. Witt: Lessons learnt from Applying AI to the Web, *Journal of Cooporative Information Systems*, 9(4), 2000.

[Fensel et al., 2000(b)]
D. Fensel, I. Horrocks, F. Van Harmelen, S. Decker, M. Erdmann, and M. Klein: OIL in a nutshell. In *Knowledge Acquisition, Modeling, and Management, Proceedings of the European Knowledge Acquisition Conference (EKAW–2000)*, R. Dieng et al. (eds.), Lecture Notes in Artificial Intelligence (LNAI 1937), Springer, October 2000.

[Fensel et al., 2001]
D. Fensel, I. Horrocks, F. van Harmelen, D. McGuinness, and P. F. Patel-Schneider: OIL: Ontology Infrastructure to Enable the Semantic Web, *IEEE Intelligent System*, 16(2), 2001.

[Fensel et al., 2002(a)]
D. Fensel, B. Omelayenko, Y. Ding, E. Schulten, G. Botquin, M. Brown, and A. Flett: *Intelligent Information Integration in B2B Electronic Commerce*, Kluwer Academic, 2002.

[Fensel et al., 2002(b)]
D. Fensel, C. Bussler, Y. Ding, B. Omelayenko: The Web Service Modeling Framework WSMF, *Electronic Commerce Research and Applications*, 1(2), 2002.

[Fensel et al., 2002(c)]
D. Fensel et al.: On-To-Knowledge: Semantic Web Enabled Knowledge Management, *IEEE Computer*, 35(11), 2002.

[Fensel et al., 2003]
D. Fensel, J. Hendler, H. Lieberman, and W. Wahlster (eds.): *Spinning the Semantic Web: Bringing the World Wide Web to Its Full Potential*, MIT Press, 2003.

[Finin et al., 1997]
T. Finin, Y. Labrou, and J. Mayfield: KQML as an agent communication language. In J. Bradshaw (ed.), *Software Agents*, MIT Press, Cambridge, MA, 1997.

[FIPA 98, part 12]
Foundation for Intelligent Physical Agents (FIPA): FIPA 98 Specification, Part 12, Ontology Service, October 1998. http://www.fipa.org.

[Fox et al., 1993]
M. S. Fox, J. F. Chionglo, and F. G. Fadel: A common sense model of the enterprise. In

Proceedings of the 2nd Industrial Engineering Research Conference, Norcross, GA, USA, 1993.

[Fox & Gruninger, 1997]
M. S. Fox and M. Gruninger: on ontologies and enterprise modelling. In *Proceedings of the International Conference on Enterprise Integration Modelling Technology'97*, Springer, 1997.

[Fridman-Noy & Hafner, 1997]
N. Fridman-Noy and C. D. Hafner: The State of the Art in Ontology Design, *AI Magazine*, 18(3):53–74, 1997.

[Van Gelder et al., 1991]
A. Van Gelder, K. Ross, and J. S. Schlipf: The well–founded semantics for general logic programs, *Journal of the ACM*, 38(3): 620–650, 1991.

[Genesereth, 1991]
M. R. Genesereth: Knowledge Interchange Format. In *Proceedings of the Second International Conference on the Principles of Knowledge Representation and Reasoning (KR–91)*, J. Allenet et. al. (eds), Morgan Kaufmann, 1991, pp. 238–249. See also http://logic.stanford.edu/kif/kif.html.

[Genesereth & Fikes, 1992]
M. R. Genesereth and R. E. Fikes: Knowledge Interchange Format, Version 3.0, Reference Manual. Technical Report, Logic-92-1, Computer Science Dept., Stanford University, 1992. http://www.cs.umbc.edu/kse.

[Glushko et al., 1999]
R. J. Glushko, J. M. Tenenbaum, and B. Meltzer: An XML framework for agent-based E–commerce, *Communications of the ACM*, 42(3), 1999.

[Gomez Perez & Benjamins, 2002]
A. Gomez-Perez and V. R. Benjamins (eds.): *Knowledge Engineering and Knowledge Management. Ontologies and the Semantic Web*, Springer, 2002.

[Greenwald & Kephart, 1999]
A. R. Greenwald and J. O. Kephart: Shopbots and pricebots. In *Proceedings of the 16th International Joint Conference on AI (IJCAI–99)*, Stockholm, Sweden, July 31–August 6, 1999.

[Grosso et al., 1999]
W. E. Grosso, H. Erikson, R. W. Fergerson, J. H. Gennari, S. W. Tu, and M. A. Musen: Knowledge modeling at the millennium (the design and evolution of Protégé-2000). In *Proceedings of the Twelfth Workshop on Knowledge Acquisition, Modeling and Management (KAW99)*, Banff, Alberta, Canada, October 16–21, 1999.

[Gruber, 1993]
T. R. Gruber: A translation approach to portable ontology specifications, *Knowledge Acquisition*, 5:199–220, 1993.

[Guarino, 1998]
N. Guarino (ed.): *Formal Ontology in Information Systems*, IOS Press, Amsterdam, 1998.

[Guha, 1993]
R. V. Guha: *Context Dependence of Representations in Cyc*, MCC Technical Report, CYC 066–93, 1993.

[Guha et al., 1998]
R. V. Guha, O. Lassila, E. Miller, and D. Brickley: Enabling inferencing. In [QL, 1998].

[Hagel & Singer, 1999]
J. Hagel III and M. Singer: *Net Worth. Shapping Markets When Customers Make the Rules*, Havard Business School Press, Boston, MA, USA, 1999.

[van Harmelen & van der Meer, 1999]
F. van Harmelen and J. van der Meer: WebMaster: Knowledge-based verification of web-pages. In *Proceedings of the Second International Conference on The Practical*

Applications of Knowledge Management (PAKeM99), London, UK, April 1999, pp. 147–166.

[van Heijst et al., 1997]
G. van Heijst, A. Schreiber, and B. Wielinga: Using Explicit Ontologies in KBS Development, *International Journal of Human-Computer Studies*, 46:183–292, 1997.

[Horrocks & Patel-Schneider, 1999]
I. Horrocks and P. F. Patel-Schneider: Optimising Description Logic Subsumption, *Journal of Logic and Computation*, 9(3):267–293, 1999.

[Hunter & Armstrong, 1999]
J. Hunter and L. Armstrong: A comparison of schemas for video metadata representation. In *Proceedings of the Eighth International World Wide Web Conference (WWW8)*, Toronto, Canada, May 11–14, 1999.

[ISO/IEC, 1990]
ISO/IEC 10027 IRDS Framework, 1990.

[ISO/IEC, 1995(a)]
ISO/IEC 10746 Reference Model of Open Distributed Processing, 1995.

[ISO/IEC, 1995(b)]
ISO/IEC 11179 Information Technology-Specification and Standardization of Data Elements, 1995.

[Jannink et al., 1998]
J. Jannink, S. Pichai, D. Verheijen, and G. Wiederhold: Encapsulation and composition of ontologies. In *Proceedings of the AAAI'98 Workshop on AI and Information Integration*, Madison, WI, July 26–27, 1998.

[Jarke et al., 2002]
M. Jarke, M. Lenzerini, Y. Vassillio, and P. Vassiliadis (eds.): *Fundamentals of Data Warehouses*, 2nd edition, Sprinber, 2002.

[Joachims et al., 1997]
T. Joachims, D. Freitag, and T. Mitchell: WebWatcher. A tour guide for the world wide web. In *Proceedings of the 15th International Joint Conference on AI (IJCAI-97)*, Nagoya, Japan, August 1997.

[Karp et al., 1999]
P. D. Karp, V. K. Chaudhri, and J. Thomere: XOL: An XML-based ontology exchange language, Version 0.3, July 3, 1999.

[Kent, 1999]
R. E. Kent: Conceptual knowledge markup language. In *Proceedings of the Twelfth Workshop on Knowledge Acquisition, Modeling and Management (KAW99)*, Banff, Canada, October 1999.

[Kifer et al., 1995]
M. Kifer, G. Lausen, and J. Wu: Logical foundations of object-oriented and frame-based languages, *Journal of the ACM*, 42, 1995.

[Kifer & Lozinskii, 1986]
M. Kifer and E. Lozinskii: A framework for an efficient implementation of deductive databases. In *Proceedings of the 6th Advanced Database Symposium*, Tokyo, 1986.

[Klein et al., 2000]
M. Klein, D. Fensel, F. van Harmelen, and I. Horrocks: The relation between ontologies and schema languages: translating OIL-specifications to XML schema In: *Proceedings of the Workshop on Applications of Ontologies and Problem-solving Methods, 14th European Conference on Artificial Intelligence ECAI-00*, Berlin, Germany, August 20–25, 2000.

[Klein et al., 2002]
M. Klein, A. Kiryakov, and D. Fensel: Finding and characterizing changes in ontologies. In *Proceedings of the 21th International Conference on Conceptual Modeling (ER2002)*, Tampere, Finland, October 2002.

[Klein et al., 2003]
M. Klein, J. Broekstra, D. Fensel, F. van Harmelen, and I. Horrocks: Ontologies and schema languages on the web. In D. Fensel et al. (eds.), *Spinning the Semantic Web: Bringing the World Wide Web to Its Full Potential*, MIT Press, Boston, 2003.

[Klusch, 1999]
M. Klusch (ed.): *Intelligent Information Agents: Agent-Based Information Discovery and Management on the Internet*, Springer, 1999.

[Krulwich, 1996]
B. Krulwich: The BargainFinder agent: Comparison price shopping on the Internet. In *Agents, Bots, and other Internet Beasties, SAMS.NET publishing*, pp. 257–263, May 1996. See also http://bf.cstar.ac.com/bf.

[Krulwich, 1997]
B. Krdlwich: Lifestyle Finder. Intelligent User profiling using large-scale demographic data, *AI Magazine*, 18(2), 1997.

[Kushmerick, 1997]
N. Kushmerick: *Wrapper induction for information extraction*. Ph.D. Dissertation, Department of Computer Science & Engineering, University of Washington, 1997. Available as Technical Report UW-CSE-97-11-04.

[Labrou & Finin, 1995]
Y. Labrou and T. Finin: Comments on the specification for FIPA'97 Agent Communication Language, University of Maryland, Baltimore County, Baltimore, MD, USA, February 28, 1997.
See http://www.cs.umbc.edu/kqml/papers/fipa/comments.shtml

[Lamping et al., 1995]
L. Lamping, R. Rao, and P. Pirolli: A focus+context technique based on hyperbolic geometry for visualizing large hierarchies. In *Proceedings of the ACM SIGCHI Conference on Human Factors in Computing Systems,* 1995.

[Lassila & Swick, 1999]
O. Lassila and R. Swick. Resource Description Framework (RDF). W3C proposed recommendation, January 1999. http://www.w3c.org/TR/WD-rdf-syntax.

[Lawrence & Giles, 1998]
S. Lawrence and C. L. Giles: Searching the world wide web, *Science*, 280(4):98–100, 1998.

[Lemahieu, 2001]
W. Lemahieu: Web service description, advertising and discovery: WSDL and beyond, 2001. In J. Vandenbulcke and M. Snoeck (eds.), *New Directions in Software Engineering,* Leuven University Press, 2001.

[Lenat, submitted]
D. B. Lenat: The Dimensions of Context Space, submitted.
http://casbah.org/resources/cycContextSpace.shtml.

[Lenat & Guha, 1990]
D. B. Lenat and R. V. Guha: *Building large knowledge-based systems. Representation and inference in the Cyc project*, Addison-Wesley, 1990.

[Leymann, 2001]
F. Leymann: Web Service Flow Language (WSFL 1.0), May 2001.
http:// www-4.ibm.com/software/solutions/webservices/pdf/WSFL.pdf.

[Li, 2000]
H. Li: XML and industrial standards for electronic commerce, *Knowledge and Information Systems: An International Journal*, 2(4), 2000.

[Lieberman, 1998(a)]
H. Lieberman: Integrating user interface agents with conventional applications, *ACM Conference on Intelligent User Interfaces*, San Fransisco, USA, January 1998.

[Lieberman, 1998b]
H. Lieberman: Beyond information retrieval: information agents at the MIT Media Lab, *Künstliche Intelligenz*, 3/98:17–23.

[Lloyd & Topor, 1984]
J. W. Lloyd and R. W: Topor: Making Prolog more expressive, *Journal of Logic Programming*, 3:225–240, 1984.

[Lopez et al., 1999]
M. F. Lopez, A. Gomez-Perez, J. P. Sierra, and A. P. Sierra: Building a chemical ontology using methontology and the ontology design environment, *Intelligent Systems*, 14(1):37–45, January/February 1999.

[Luke et al., 1996]
S. Luke, L. Spector, and D. Rager: Ontology-based knowledge discovery on the world-wide web. In *Proceedings of the Workshop on Internet-based Information Systems at the AAAI-96*, Portland, Oregon, USA, August 4–8, 1996.

[Luke et al. 1997]
S. Luke, L. Spector, D. Rager, and J. Hendler. Ontology-based Web agents. In *First International Conference on Autonomous Agents (AA'97)*, 1997.

[MacGregor, 1994]
R. MacGregor: A description classifier for the predicate calculus. In *Proceedings of the 12th National Conference on AI (AAAI-94)*, pp. 213–220, 1994.

[Maedche, 2002]
A. Maedche: *Ontology Learning for the Semantic Web*, The Kluwer International Series in Engineering and Computer Science, Volume 665, Kluwer Academic, 2002.

[Maes et al., 1999]
P. Maes, R. H. Guttman, and A. G. Moukas: Agent, that buy and sell, *Communications of the ACM*, 42(3), March 1999.

[Malhotra & Maloney, 1999]
A. Malhotra and M. Maloney: XML Schema Requirements. W3C Note, February 1999. http://www.w3.org/TR/NOTE-xml-schema-req.

[Manola, 1998]
F. Manola: Towards a web object model, In *Pro-ceedings of the Workshop on Compositional Software Architectures*, Monterey, CA, USA, January 6–8, 1998.

[McCarthy 1993]
J. McCarthy: Notes on formalizing context. In *Proceedings of the 13th International Conference on Artificial Intelligence (IJCAI-93)*, Chambery, France, 1993.

[McEntire et al., 1999]
R. McEntire, P. Karp, N. Abernethy, F. Olken, R. E. Kent, M. DeJongh, P. Tarczy-Hornoch, D. Benton, D. Pathak, G. Helt, S. Lewis, A. Kosky, E. Neumann, D. Hodnett, L. Tolda, and T. Topaloglou: *An Evaluation of Ontology Exchange Languages for Bioinformatics*, August 1999.

[McGuinness, 1999]
D. L. McGuinness: Ontologies for electronic commerce. In *Proceedings of the AAAI '99 Artificial Intelligence for Electronic Commerce Workshop*, Orlando, FL, USA, July 1999.

[McGuinness et al., 2000]
D. L. McGuinness, R. Fikes, J. Rice, and S. Wilder: The Chimaera ontology environment. In the *Proceedings of the The Seventeenth National Conference on Artificial Intelligence (AAAI 2000)*, Austin, TX, USA, July 30–August 3, 2000.

[McGuinness et al., 2002]
D. L. McGuinness, R. Fikes, J. Hendler, and L. A. Stein: DAML+OIL: An ontology language for the semantic web, *IEEE Intelligent Systems*, 17(5), 2002.

[McGuinness & van Harmelen, 2002]
D. L. McGuinness and F. van Harmelen: Feature Synopsis for OWL Lite and OWL,

W3C Working Draft 29 July 2002.
http://www.w3.org/TR/2002/WD-owl-features-20020729.

[Meersman, 2000]
R. A. Meersman: The use of lexicons and other computer-linguistic tools in semantics, design and cooperation of database systems. In Y. Zhang (ed.), *CODAS Conference Proceedings,* Springer, 2000.

[Microsoft (a)]
Microsoft: *Open Information Model.* http://msdn.microsoft.com/repository/OIM and http://www.mdcinfo.com/OIM.

[Microsoft (b)]
Microsoft: *XML Interchange Format (XIF).* http://msdn.microsoft.com/repository.

[Miller, 1998]
E. Miller: An introduction to the Resource Description Framework, *D-Lib Magazine,* May 1998.

[Muslea et al., 1998]
I. Muslea, S. Minton, and C. Knoblock: Wrapper induction for semistructured, web-based information sources. In *Proceedings of the Conference on Automatic Learning and Discovery*, Pennsylvania, USA, Pittsburgh, 1998.

[Muslea et al., 1998]
B. Nebel: Artificial Intelligence: a computational perspective. In G. Brewka (ed.), *Principles of Knowledge Representation*, CSLI publications, Stanford, 1996.

[Noy & Musen, 2000]
N. F. Noy and M. Musen: PROMPT: Algorithm and tool for automated ontology merging and alignment. In *Proceedings of the Seventeenth National Conference on Artificial Intelligence (AAAI-2000)*, Austin, TX, 2000. AAAI/MIT Press.
http://www-smi.stanford.edu/pubs/SMI_Reports/SMI-2000-0831.pdf.

[Nwana, 1996]
H. S. Nwana: Software Agents: an overview, *Knowledge Engineering Review*, 11(3), 1996.

[O'Leary, 1997]
D. E O'Leary: The Internet, intranets, and the AI renaissance, *IEEE Intelligent Systems*, January 1997.

[Omelayenko et al., 2002]
B. Omelayenko, D. Fensel, and C. Bussler: Mapping technology for enterprise integration. In *Proceedings of the 15th International FLAIRS Conference*, AAAI Press, Pensacola, FL, May 16–18, 2002.

[Omelayenko & Fensel, 2001]
B. Omelayenko and D. Fensel: a two-layered integration approach for product information in B2B e-commerce. In K. Bauknechjt et al. (eds.), *Electronic Commerce and Web Technology*, Lecture Notes in Computer Science (LNCS 2115), Springer, 2001, pp. 226–239.

[OMG, 1997]
Object Management Group (OMG): Meta Object Facility (MOF) Specification, 1997.

[OMG, 1998]
Object Management Group (OMG): Stream-Based Model Interchange, 1998.

[Peat & Webber, 1997]
B. Peat and D. Webber: XML/EDI – the E-business framework, August 1997, http://www.geocities.com/WallStreet/Floor/5815/startde.htm.

[Perkowitz & Etzioni, 1997]
M. Perkowitz and O. Etzioni: Adaptive web sites: an AI challenge. In *Proceedings of the 15th International Joint Conference on AI (IJCAI-97)*, Nagoya, Japan, August 23–29, 1997.

[Perkowitz & Etzioni, 1999]
M. Perkowitz and O. Etzioni: Adaptive web sites: conceptual clustering mining. In *Proceedings of the 16th International Joint Conference on AI (IJCAI-99)*, Stockholm, Sweden, July 31–August 6, 1999.

[Puerta et al., 1992]
A. R. Puerta, J. W. Egar, S. W. Tu, and M. A.Musen: A multiple-method knowledge acquisition shell for the automatic generation of knowledge acquisition tools, *Knowledge Acquisition*, 4(2):171–196, 1992.

[QL, 1998]
Proceedings of W3C Query Language Workshop (QL'98) – The Query Languages Workshop, Boston, MA, USA, December 3–4, 1998.
http://www.w3.org/TandS/QL/QL98.

[Rabarijoana et al., 1999]
A. Rabarijoana, R. Dieng, and O. Corby: Exploitation of XML for corporative knowledge management. In D. Fensel and R. Studer (eds.), *Knowledge Acquisition, Modeling, and Management, Proceedings of the European Knowledge Acquisition Workshop (EKAW-99)*, Lecture Notes in Artificial Intelligence (LNAI 1621), Springer, 1999.

[Sakata et al., 1997]
T. Sakata, H. Tada, and T. Ohtake: Metadata mediation: representation and protocol. In *Proceedings of the 6th International World Wide Web Conference (WWW6)*, Santa Clara, California, USA, April 7–11, 1997.

[Selberg & Etzioni, 1997]
M. Selberg and O. Etzioni: The Metacrawler architecture for resource aggregation on the Web, *IEEE Expert*, January–February 1997.

[Shardanand & Maes, 1995]
U. Shardanand and P. Maes: Social information filtering: algorithms for automating "word of mouth". In *Proceedings of the SIG Computer and Human Interaction, ACM Press*, New York, 1995.

[Staudt et al., 1999]
M. Staudt, A. Vaduva, and T. Vetterli: Metadata management and data warehousing, Swiss Life, Information Systems Research, Technical Report no. 21, 1999.
http://research.swisslife.ch/Papers/data/smart/meta.ps.

[Studer et al., 1996]
R. Studer, H. Eriksson, J. H. Gennari, S. W. Tu, D. Fensel, and M. Musen: Ontologies and the configuration of problem-solving methods. In B. R. Gaines and M. A. Musen, (eds.), *Proceedings of the 10th Banff Knowledge Acquisition for Knowledge-Based Systems Workshop*, Banff, Canada, 1996.

[Sure et al., 2002]
Y. Sure, M. Erdmann, J. Angele, S. Staab, R. Studer, and D. Wenke: OntoEdit: collaborative ontology engineering for the semantic web. In I. Horrocks and J. Hendler (eds.), *The Semantic Web – ISWC 2002, Proceedings of the First International Semantic Web Conference*, Sardinia, Italy, June 9–12, 2002, Lecture Notes in Computer Science (LNCS 2342), Springer, 2002.

[Swartout et al., 1996]
B. Swartout, R. Patil, K. Knight, and T. Russ: Toward dsistributed use of large-scale ontologies. In B. R. Gaines and M. A. Musen, (eds.), *Proceedings of the 10th Banff Knowledge Acquisition for Knowledge-Based Systems Workshop*, Banff, Canada, 1996.

[Sycara et al., 1999]
K. Sycara, J. Lu, M. Klusch, and S. Widoff: Matchmaking among heterogeneous agents on the Internet. In *Proceedings of the AAAI Spring Symposium on Intelligent Agents in Cyberspace*, Stanford, CA, USA, 1999.

[Trastour et al., 2001]
D. Trastour, C. Bartolini, and J. Gonzalez-Castillo: A semantic web approach to service

description for matchmaking of services. In *Proceedings of the Semantic Web Working Symposium*, Stanford, CA, USA, July 30–August 1, 2001.

[Thatte, 2001]
S. Thatte: XLANG: Web Services for Business Process Design, Microsoft Corporation, 2001. http://www.gotdotnet.com/team/xml_wsspecs/xlang-c/default.htm.

[Thompson et al., 2000]
H. S. Thompson, D. Beech, M. Maloney, and N. Mendelsohn: XML Schema Part 1: Structures, W3C Candidate Recommendation, 24 October 2000. http://www.w3.org/TR/2000/CR-xmlschema-1-20001024.

[Ullman, 1988]
J. D. Ullman: *Principles of Database and Knowledge-Base Systems*, Vol I, Computer Sciences Press, Rockville, MD, USA, 1988.

[Uschold et al., 1996]
M. Uschold, M. King, S. Moralee, and Y. Zorgio: The enterprise ontology, *Knowledge Engineering Review*, 11(2), 1996.

[Waldt & Drummond]
D. Waldt and R. Drummond: ebXML: the global standard for electronic business. http://www.ebxml.org/presentations/global_standard.htm.

[Walsh, 1999]
N. Walsh: Schemas for XML, July 1, 1999. http://www.xml.com/pub/1999/07/schemas/index.html.

[Weibel, 1999]
S. Weibel: The state of the Dublin Core Metadata Initiative April 1999, *D-Lib Magazine*, 5(4), 1999.

[Weibel et al., 1995]
S. Weibel, J. Gridby, and E. Miller: OCLC/NCSA Metadata Workshop Report, Dublin, EUA, 1995. http://www.oclc.org:5046/oclc/research/conferences/metadata/dublin_core_report.html.

[Weinstein & Birmingham, 1999]
P. C. Weinstein and W. P. Birmingham: Comparing concepts in differentiated Ontologies. In: *Proceedings of KAW'99: 12th Banff Knowledge Acquisition Workshop*, Banff, Canada, October 16–21, 1999.

[v. Westarp et al., 1999]
F. v. Westarp, T. Weitzel, P. Buxmann, and W. König: The status quo and the future of EDI–results of an empirical study. In *Proceedings of the European Conference on Information Systems (ECIS'99)*, 1999.

[Welty & Ide, 1999]
C. Welty and N. Ide: Using the right tools: enhancing retrieval from marked-up documents, *Computers and the Humanities,* 33(1–2), Special Issue on the Tenth Anniversary of the Text Encoding Initiative, 1999.

[Wiederhold, 1992]
G. Wiederhold: Mediators in the architecture of future information systems, *IEEE Computer*, 25(3):38–49, 1992.

[Wiederhold, 1997]
G. Wiederhold: Value-added mediation in large-scale information systems. In R. Meersman and L. Mark (eds.): *Database Application Semantics*, Chapman and Hall, 1997, pp. 34–56.

[Wiederhold & Genesereth, 1997]
G. Wiederhold and M. Genesereth: The conceptual basis for mediation services. *IEEE Expert*, pp. 38–47, September/October 1997.

Abbreviations

API	Application Programming Interface
ASCII	American Standard Code for Information Interchange
ASP	Active Server Pages
B2B	Business-to-Business
B2C	Business-to-Consumer
BPEL4WS	Business Process Execution Language for Web Services
BNB	British National Bibliography
BPML	Business Process Modeling Language
BPSS	Business Process Specification Schema
CBL	Common Business Library
CDIF	Case Data Interchange Format
CGI	Common Gateway Interface
CKML	Conceptual Knowledge Markup Language
CML	Conceptual Modeling Language)
CORBA	Common Object Request Broker Architecture
CPC	United Nations Common Procurement Code
CRM	Customer Relationship Management
CSS	Cascading Stylesheet
CVS	Current Versioning System
cXML	Commerce XML
DAML	DARPA Agent Markup Language
DAML-S	DAML Services
DARPA	Defense Advanced Research Projects Agency
DCD	Document Content Description for XML
DCOM	Distributed Component Object Model
DL	Description Logics
DDL	Data Definition Language
DLL	Dynamic Link Library
DLP	Description Logic Prover
DSig	Digital Signature Working Group
DTD	Document Type Definition
DSSSL	Document Style Semantics and Specification Language
EAI	Enterprise Application Integration

ebXML	Electronic Business using XML
ECAI	European Conference on Artificial Intelligence
ECCMA	Electronic Commerce Code Management Association
ECMA	European Computer Manufacturers Association
EDI	Electronic Data Interchange
EDIFACT	Electronic Data Interchange for Administration, Commerce and Transport
ERP	Enterprise Resource Planning
FaCT	Fast Classification of Terminologies
FIPA	Foundation for Intelligent Physical Agents
GFP	Generic Frame Protocol
GUI	Graphical User Interface
HTML	Hypertext Markup Language
IBROW	Intelligent Brokering Service for Knowledge-Component Reuse on the WWW
ICE	Information and Content Exchange protocol
IDL	OMG Interface Definition Language
IEC	International Electrotechnical Commission
IEEE	Institute of Electrical and Electronics Engineers, Inc.
IETF	Internet Engineering Task Force
<indecs>	Interoperability of Data in E-Commerce Systems
IOTP	Internet Open Trading Protocol
IRDS	Information Resource Dictionary System
ISO	International Organization for Standardization
IST	Information Society Technology
JSP	Java Server Pages
$(KA)^2$	Knowledge Annotation Initiative of the Knowledge Acquisition Community
KIF	Knowledge Interchange Format
KQML	Knowledge Query and Manipulation Language
MARC	Machine Readable Code Record Format
MIT	Massachusetts Institute of Technology
MOF	Meta Object Facility
MPEG	Moving Picture Experts Group
NAICS	North American Industry Classification System
OAG	Open Applications Group
OAGIS	Open Applications Group Integration Specification
OBI	Open Buying on the Internet
OCF	Open Catalog Format
ODE	Ontology Design Environment
ODL	ODMG Object Definition

ODMG	Object Data Management Group
ODP	Open Distributed Processing
OFX	Open Financial Exchange
OIL	Ontology Inference Layer
OIM	Open Information Model
OMG	Object Management Group
OML	Ontology Markup Language
OKBC	Open Knowledge Base Connectivity
OMM	Ontology Middleware Module
OWL	Web Ontology Language
P3P	Platform for Privacy Preferences Project
PCTE	Portable Common Tool Environment
PHP	Hypertext Preprocessor
PI	Processing Instruction
PICS	Platform for Internet Content Selection
PIP	Partner Interface Process
RDF	Resource Description Framework
RDFS	Resource Description Framework Schema
RDFT	RDF Transformations
RETML	Real Estate Transaction Markup Language
RM-ODP	Reference Model of Open Distributed Processing
RMI	Remote Method Invocation
RPC	Remote Procedure Call
RQL	RDF Query Language
TOVE	Toronto Virtual Enterprise
SGML	Standard Generalized Markup Language
SHOE	Simple HTML Ontology Extensions
SiLRI	Simple Logic-based RDF Interpreter
SKC	Scalable Knowledge Composition
SOAP	Simple Object Access Protocol
SOIF	Summary Object Interchange Format
SOX	Schema for Object-Oriented XML
SPSC	Standard Product and Service Codes
SQL	Structured Query Language
SWSC	International Joint Semantic Web Services ad hoc Consortium
SWWS	Semantic Web enabled Web Services
TCP/IP	Transfer Control Protocol/Internet Protocol
TEI	Text Encoding Initiative
UDDI	Universal Description, Discovery, and Integration
UML	Unified Modeling Language

UNCCS	United Nations Common Coding System
UN/CEFACT	United Nations Centre for Trade Facilitation and Electronic Business
UN/SPSC	United Nations Standard Products and Services Code
UPML	Unified Problem-solving Method description Language
URI	Uniform Resource Identifiers
URL	Uniform Resource Locator
W3C	World Wide Web Consortium
WfMC	Workflow Management Coalition
WPDL	Workflow Process Definition Language
WSCL	Web Services Conversation Language
WSDL	Web Service Description Language
WSFL	Web Services Flow Language
WSIL	Web Service Inspection Language
WSMF	Web Service Modeling Framework
WWW	World Wide Web
xCBL	XML Common Business Library
XIF	XML Interchange Facility
XMI	XML Metadata Interchange
XML	Extensible Markup Language
XML-QL	XML Query Language
XOL	XML-based Ontology Exchange Language
XSL	Extensible Style Language
XSLT	XSL Transformations

Index

Druck: Strauss Offsetdruck, Mörlenbach
Verarbeitung: Schäffer, Grünstadt